WALK INTO YOUR SEASON

WALK INTO YOUR SEASON

The Art of Cultural Work

Peyton McCoy, Ph.D.

Foreword by Richard Couto, PhD
Cover Photgraphy by Frank Anderson

iUniverse, Inc.
Bloomington

Walk into Your Season
The Art of Cultural Work

iUniverse books may be ordered through booksellers or by contacting:

iUniverse
1663 Liberty Drive
Bloomington, IN 47403
www.iuniverse.com
1-800-Authors (1-800-288-4677)

Because of the dynamic nature of the Internet, any web addresses or links contained in this book may have changed since publication and may no longer be valid. The views expressed in this work are solely those of the author and do not necessarily reflect the views of the publisher, and the publisher hereby disclaims any responsibility for them.

Any people depicted in stock imagery provided by Thinkstock are models, and such images are being used for illustrative purposes only.

Certain stock imagery © Thinkstock.

ISBN: 978-1-4759-8307-4 (sc)
ISBN: 978-1-4759-8309-8 (hc)
ISBN: 978-1-4759-8308-1 (e)

Library of Congress Control Number: 2013905363

Printed in the United States of America

iUniverse rev. date: 04/11/2013

Contents

Acknowledgments

Time and space do not allow detailed expressions of thanks to the many people who were instrumental in making this project come to fruition. I am thankful for the patience, attentiveness, focus, and dedication that countless individuals poured into my life, my work, and the *Walk into Your Season* vision.

I am thankful, awed, and inspired by the spirit of my parents, Robert and Ellen Baker ("Little Debbie") McCoy, who sacrificed so much in order that I might dream, learn, experiment, explore, and express myself. I am so proud to be your daughter. I am also proud to be the granddaughter of Lucy Peyton Baker; the great niece of Mary E. Peyton, who was blind from birth yet taught me to read using stories with Braille text on one side and printed text on the other; and the niece of my moxie "Aunt Kate" Baker Collins and the ever so humorous Lina Nett McCoy Casper (Aunt Nett). Memories continue to carve a creative space where cultural legacy, intellect, wisdom, and kindred souls clap hands and sing new songs.

Walk into Your Season is a token of gratitude in memory of the help rendered and the gifts empowered by Dr. Darrel Rollins (Thirty-First Street Baptist Church) and Dr. Stephen Lenton (Virginia Commonwealth University). It is true—the good that men do does indeed live after them as does the unconditional faith they invest in an individual's unrealized potential.

I owe a tremendous debt of gratitude to Dr. Wyatt Tee Walker and his wife, Mrs. Ann Walker who were so gracious in supporting *Walk into Your Season*, encouraging me to stay the course, inviting me into their home, and answering my questions about their work in the civil rights movement. I treasure those conversations, Dr. and Mrs. Walker's visits to Thirty-First Street, and everything they did so that I and others could walk into a new season of expanded opportunities.

Though I am an only child, my parents' neighbors George and Celestine Hardy (and their children Gina, Sheryl, George, and Phyllis) made sure that I never felt like one. Thank you for always calling me "one of your children," as you toted me to the Portsmouth Public Library and to your family outings with your own children. Thank you for loving me through good times, tough times, and vulnerable times.

To the members of academic community, words seem paltry at moments like this. You set the bar at a high level on multiple dimensions. Then your firm guidance, scholarly demeanor, attentiveness, and commitment to my vision allowed me to reach the bar:

Dr. Richard Couto (committee chairman), I will never forget our long talks, lunches at Lucille's, and challenging yet thought-provoking discussions about *Walk into Your Season*. (Nor will I forget my quick chats with Mrs. Couto and her consistent kindness in making sure you received my messages.) However, it is the depth and breadth of your scholarship, your incisive and decisive writing, your numerous books exemplifying this masterful craftsmanship (I stopped counting after nineteen), your wit, and your relentless resolve to listen and get it right that are now stitched into my memories. Every day, I think about how richly I have benefited from your impeccable scholarship; but the dearest observation I take away is your ability to walk with kings and never lose the common touch. Your humble spirit is reassuring in a complex world of people long on ego yet short on vision. Thank you for all that you have done for me; most of all, thanks for being you and allowing me to observe excellence personified.

Dr. Elden Golden, you were one of the first to believe in this project. Thank you for raising the bar on creativity and inspiring me to make the implicit explicit. You inspired me to think, rethink, and then think again. Your encouragement, scholarly knowledge of creativity as a process, a product, and a place, alongside your willingness to think outside the box within the realm of scholarship made all the difference. Thanks for always taking the time to envision the end and then (re)considering how I might get there.

Dr. Norma Jenckes, thank you for embracing my nascent gifts from the very start—my very first day at The Union Institute. Then too, thank you for challenging me to stay true to myself and the work. You reminded me that this was my work and if it came to making a choice between the scholarly safety zone and the passion and exhilaration of scholarly exploration—the latter was the high road that would provide sustenance for the long haul. You were right.

Thanks to the entire Union Institute staff for every act of support, kindness, and encouragement. I am indebted to former dean Larry Preston and interim dean Karsten Piep for their willingness to engage my thoughts and support my work. I am thankful for the sound judgment, kind demeanor, and meticulous care of Dr. Toni Gregory. Though a mere thank you seems insufficient, please know that your guidance will illuminate my thinking for a lifetime.

I am also indebted to Senior Pastor Dr. Morris Henderson, the official boards, and the Thirty-First Street Baptist Church Family, the Richmond Department of Social Services, the respective focus group participants of Walk into Your Season, the Walk into Your Season program participants, the staff of the Children's Museum, former colleagues at the Virginia Department of Social Services, and the Richmond Alumnae Chapter of Delta Sigma Theta Sorority, Inc.

I appreciate some special friends and the support of their spouses. Thanks to Dr. Vivian Stith-Williams (Bob) and Dr. Jackie Joyner (Dr. William "Bill"), who can at once inject sisterhood, friendship, and scholarship into one sentence; Deacon Larry Kearney, who kept on praying and then some; Frank Anderson and Rob Dungee, for lending their impeccable talents with photography, audiovisuals and sound in the public Walk into Your Season programs, and for being extraordinary friends; my former manager Letha Moore-Jones (Rev. Bruce) for supporting my vision; and Mrs. Naomi Brodie, for keeping all the scheduling details straight and a million other things.

Finally, last but by no means least, I am thankful for a small group of friends and their families who helped at moments when they perhaps did not even realize it. They are my extended family circle. Their words, actions, support, understanding, and commitment (even when they could not have possibly been sure of the end product) allowed me to experience extended family in a soul deep, mountain-wide, marvelous way. This circle surrounds me with their gifts, humor, love, and devotion. Special thanks to the following:

Evelyn Murphy (Bill), I am proud to be your daughter sister child; Shelia Spurlock-Shaw (Thomas and Gladys); Patsy Logan (Everett and Jay); Howard and Sylvia Spurlock (Jada, Kelly, and Jaelyn); Norman and Betty Jackson (Marshell and Cory), Gina Hardy-Harris (Warren and Warren), my confidant since I was four years old; cousins Betty Toadvine-Moore (Lewis) and George Tyler (Patsy, in loving memory); and Linda Brown, Pearl Wise-Crawley, Ingrid Crump, Stephanie Miller, and G. D. Stevens. Thanks for being my friends through the years. Our journey through the years gives me hope, strength, and excitement for a new season due to the emergent wisdom and love perpetually renewed in the old. Thank you for allowing me to be your friend so that I might benefit from your soul deep transforming love in this, a new season.

Peyton

Foreword

Richard A. Couto
Distinguished Senior Scholar
Union Institute and University

In this highly original work, Peyton McCoy takes the aspirations of bell hooks and Cornell West for a new combination of artistry, scholarship, and social justice; puts these aspirations into practice as a cultural work; reflects on her experience; and then sheds light on the path to cultural work for others who would follow. This is quite an achievement and an extraordinary example of making the road by walking.

Dr. McCoy brings tacit knowledge and reflective practice into her work. She is a member of the two communities in which she conducted this cultural work; the Thirty-First Street Baptist Church in Richmond, Virginia, and the transition program of the foster care department of the Virginia Department of Social Work. She does not try to explain those communities to outsiders or to themselves through her experience within them as in the case of field work or ethnography. Rather, her cultural draws from their cultural legacy about which she has tacit knowledge and upon which she reflects critically to portray the communities' assets of resistance and empowerment.

As interesting and important as her two events are, Dr. McCoy also offers readers a thoughtful synthesis of literature, philosophy, and several branches of social science to explain the concepts of her work. Langston Hughes, Toni Morrison, and Henrik Ibsen and many other literary luminaries join philosophers Cornel West, Jurgen Habermas, and Michel Foucault and social science scholars such as Donald Schoen, James Scott, and Mihaly Csikszentmihalyi as Dr. McCoy brings together the related insights from disparate sources that inform her work. The synapses of the connections that she makes crackle across the pages of her work.

In theory and practice, these pages gracefully explain cultural work as an art form built from the repertoire of experiences that the community members share. In her two different and distinct presentations, Dr. McCoy wove photos, music, biography, and testimonials together with narrative poetry. The presentation in the Thirty-First Street Baptist Church, which I attended, sought to recall, explain, and renew the role of the black church as a free space in which people met as a discursive community and found the assets and resources among themselves to take on the challenges around them. Ever the innovator, Dr. McCoy took the idea of cultural work one step further to initiate, rather than renew, a free space of empowerment within a discursive community, the transition program for foster children.

Dr. McCoy's pioneering effort on cultural work has profound implications for leadership and addresses three paradigmatic challenges in the study and practice of leadership. The first two deal with the purpose of leadership.

Robert Greenleaf developed his concept of servant leadership as an antidote to the mediocrity he saw in United States social institutions—corporate, educational, government, religious, foundations, and others (Greenleaf 1977, 247–48). His remedy for institutional mediocrity revolves about trusteeship within them. When Greenleaf was an undergraduate, a professor planted in his mind the growing importance of large institutions in the economic and social fabric of the United States and the idea of working for good inside of them. As an adult, he came to understand the increased likelihood of people having careers within large organizations; he worked most of his life in ATT. The 1960s displayed the fragility of these organizations and their failure to meet their higher social purposes with the resources that they had. Greenleaf felt compelled to do something to turn institutions toward greatness through legitimate power of institutions within the people who worked in them.

His reflections on leadership aim to build organizations that serve and lead and to assist individuals within them to do the same. He asserts that the desire to serve must precede the ambition the achieve leadership positions. His hope and prescription for organizational and individual renewal that promote social purpose and benefit appeals to us still and has shaped the turn of leadership studies, in style and content, that Joseph Rost detected after 1980 (1993, 2). CEOs have endorsed servant leadership in their reflections on their leadership experience (DePree 1990; George 2003, 19). Servant leadership and cultural work have several similarities in their efforts to "renew or initiate free space in a discursive community with consequences for empowerment." Most of all, cultural work may be effective in reminding people about their trusteeship for the social and moral purposes of the group or institution or which they may be a part.

At the same time that Greenleaf wrote, James MacGregor Burns also turned to leadership, transforming leadership, as a remedy to the mediocrity he observed a decade after the hopes and aspirations for social justice of the 1960s. Burns informs his readers that transforming leadership "is a relationship of mutual stimulation and elevation that converts followers into leaders and may convert leaders into moral agents" (1978, 4). Burns offers another definition later in the book when he explains that transforming leadership "occurs when one or more persons *engage* with others in such a way that leaders and followers raise one another to higher levels of motivation and morality" (1978, 20). The test of transforming leadership, for Burns, comes from social movements. "Significant change" entails the abolition of some caste-like restriction that impaired the recognition of the human worth of a group of people and the public expression of their values and needs. Transforming leadership, like cultural work, entails a group and change *within* the group and *of* and *by* the group.

Transforming leadership, Burns asserts, changes some of those who follow into people whom others may follow later. It also changes leaders into moral agents. Burns defines morality in terms of human development and of a hierarchy of human needs. He borrows from humanistic psychologists, for example Lawrence Kohlberg, Erik Erikson, and Abraham Maslow, for these terms and concepts. Transforming leadership assists a group of people to move from one stage of development to a higher one and in doing so to address and fulfill better a higher human need. The leader's fundamental act is to induce people to be aware or conscious of what they feel and to feel their true needs so strongly and to define their values so meaningfully that they can move to purposeful action (Burns 1978, 44). Among the echoes of Burns's call for moral leadership that one finds in the pages of *Walk into Your Season* is explicit reference to the same stream of psychology, now called positive rather than humanistic psychology. Moreover, cultural work seems to be an avenue to the leverage of group and institutional members to "higher levels of motivation and morality" at which they assume the responsibilities of leadership even if without formal positional authority.

This brings us to the third paradigmatic link of *Walk into Your Season* to the study of leadership: who is a leader? Using complexity theory, Mary Uhl-Bien and Russ Marion (2010) challenge the equation of leadership with leader as positional authority, or power over, in an organizational context. Complexity theory replaces the assumptions of a Newtonian world of certainty, causality, predictability and control, which support conventional concepts of leadership, with assumptions of uncertainty, self-organizations, nonlinearity, and the necessity of chaos for the emergence of transforming possibilities

(Uhl-Bien and Marion p. xvii). In complexity, "no one person completely understands or is able to fully predict the outcome of an action....Leaders are *not* really in control" (Uhl-Bien and Marion 2008, xvii–xviii). In this paradigm, leadership is "*an emergent, interactive dynamic*—a complex interplay from which a collective impetus for action and change emerges when heterogeneous agents interact in new ways that produce new patterns of behavior or new modes of operating" (Uhl-Bien, Marion, McKelvey 2010, 187). This form of leadership appeared in the social movements of the 1960s including of course the civil rights movement within which African Americans played a significant part as free spaces, discursive communities and empowerment. Dr. McCoy's cultural work intended to renew this legacy and the form of leadership that it entails.

The work of Uhl-Bien and Marion (2010) also "moves us from bureaucratic notions of control and predictability to a view of leadership in complex, adaptive, nonlinear feedback networks... [and as] an emergent, interactive process embedded in context and history (Uhl-Bien in Uhl-Bien and Marion, p. vii). Here too, Dr. McCoy leads the way by working within a social service agency to initiate this form of leadership with extensive use of its context and history. She explains the necessity of this work in terms very similar to Uhl-Bien and Marion. "The necessity ... resides in creating environments that nurture opportunities for community building, healing, identity and cultural transmission, wisdom transmission, and social capital."

From the theory of complexity we may conclude that we need a new concept of leader, if not a new word. That word would be more related to socially purposeful leadership as Greenleaf and Burns suggested. As you read the many sources that inform the concept of cultural work and the ten principles of effective cultural work, ask yourself if they are not excellent foundations and principles for the insightful study and improved practice of leadership that we seem to seek and desperately need.

References

Burns, James MacGregor. 1978. *Leadership*. New York: Harper and Row Publishers.

DePree, Max. 1990. *Leadership Is an Art*. New York: Doubleday.

George, Bill. 2003. *Authentic Leadership: Rediscovering the Secrets to Creating Lasting Value*. San Francisco: Jossey-Bass.

Greenleaf, Robert K. 1977. *Servant Leadership: A Journey into the Nature of Legitimate Power and Greatness*. New York: Paulist Press.

Rost, Joseph C. 1991. *Leadership for the Twenty-First Century*. Westport, CT: Praeger.

Uhl-Bien, M., and R. Marion. 2008. *Complexity Leadership: Part 1. Conceptual Foundations*. Charlotte, NC: Information Age.

Overview

*To my beloved community: when tough stuff hits the
fan, some folk run, but some folk take a stand.*

I was shocked. Not by the behavior—I was accustomed to that—but the rationale. It was "off the chain." The program manager was scolding me. Her tirades of epic proportion were legendary yet tolerated by people in high places in the organization. In her opinion my presentation to a group of high-level agency staff persons was unacceptable. As I mentally revisited the occasion, I remember her look of disgust as well as that of a sole colleague who sat beside her. Yet the sense of indignation did not register on the faces of the other attendees. I sensed a disconnect between her perception and that of the audience. I ran through a mental checklist to ascertain the source of her displeasure. Was it the content (surely not, as I had vetted the information with multiple members representing multiple organizational levels in a designated workgroup); was it the analysis (how could this be since I worked with the data team to crunch the numbers); was it breach of policy (well, I was not given a protocol, and efforts to obtain one, get simple answers, or just communicate met resistance)? I would soon learn that it was not my substance; it was my style.

I had been assigned a monumental task with minimal access, help, direction, or counsel. I felt like I was in a state somewhere between swimming upstream in a mudslide and scuba diving in a cesspool. Nevertheless, much success was obtained through diverse people with diverse backgrounds coming together to work on a common goal. On the other hand, the minimal accommodations afforded me a room with an expansive view to observe how the ploys of power, organizational dysfunction, and managerial personal insecurity can derail good work, sideline worthy intentions, and further oppress vulnerable people/stakeholders. In my naivety, conceiving communication to be essential to any meaningful endeavor (or at least helpful since we can facilitate and encourage yet cannot force people to communicate), I posed the question—what did I do wrong? Herein resides my shock. "Well," she responded, "you tell stories."

Thinking she was referring to content accuracy I, in escalating shock, countered, "I beg your pardon."

"You use stories in your presentations and I don't like it. There you were at a high-level meeting using stories."

I could not fathom this egregious error and unforgivable sin she portrayed. However I now know that we all encounter individuals in whose eyes we cannot even do wrong right. On the other hand, I have learned that such individuals and instances are an unexpected gift. Opportunities for deep reflection and self-discovery unfold. In a moment of uncharacteristic candor the program manager unveiled what was for me a revelation in a statement that ran contrary to her disdain. "Nevertheless," she continued, "I have learned that I can no longer ignore how people respond to those stories."

In spite of the perpetual duress she imposed, this was a thought provoking statement embedded in a notion that holds dual citizenship. My relationship with stories began in the church, but the relationship is bigger than an institution. What the manager had missed was how the meaningful use of the culturally specific simple story can connect people with an understanding of complex social issues in order to find solutions. This is an art. Managers sometimes fail to recognize what a different lens brings to problem solving in organizational culture. The oversight leads to dysfunctional, toxic mayhem. Inflammatory statements, questionable practices, power, dysfunction, and silence commingle to build the illusion of making headway at the expense of vulnerable people. Albert Einstein's belief that people come to art and science to create "a simplified and lucid image of the world," hoping in this way to attain some peace and serenity amid the cruelties of daily life, states my case. He encapsulates my sentiment and motivation regarding cultural work. *Walk into Your Season: The Art of Cultural Work* conceives cultural work as part of a broader effort that reaches beyond the individual self (yet includes the individual self), reaches across ethnicity (yet respects the lessons from ethnic groups), seeks individual and collective empowerment, and explores how to survive and thrive in the midst of (yet in spite of) dysfunctional environments. The diverse processes of expression—the ways in which individuals acquire powerful means to convey their thoughts to others—shifts from a person-centered approach to one that includes the dynamic and social aspects of creativity. I tell the story through diverse processes (graphical, musical, verbal, and images), fortified by data with an eye on problem solving and empowerment.

I employ the "power of images." I was fascinated by the physicists and mathematicians who have described the role of images in their thinking. Physicist/artist John Howarth helped me understand this abstract visualization and why a picture articulates a thousand words. I make abstract pictures, he said, and realized that the process of abstraction in the pictures in my head is similar to the abstraction you engage in dealing with physical problems analytically. You reduce the number of variables, simplify and consider what you hope is the essential part of the situation you are dealing with, then apply your analytical techniques. In making a visual picture it is possible to choose one which contains representations of only the essential elements—a simplified picture, abstracted from a number of other pictures and containing their common elements (John-Steiner 1997, 109–110). The ability of film and cinema in cultural work to represent the moving images of thought on many levels—conscious and subconscious—is exciting. It is through these languages... that viewers may experience the previously hidden links between the past and the present, the observer and the observed, and the mind and the "undermind" (137).

Walk into Your Season: The Art of Cultural Work examines the role of the cultural worker and four related factors: (a) cultural work, (b) free space, (c), discursive communities, and (d) empowerment. The cultural worker is a scholar artist, conceived as a person demonstrating the creativity of the artist, yet the intellectual rigor of a scholar. I began by illustrating the role of the "cultural worker" in two public programs entitled Walk into Your Season. I conducted these two events as cultural work using methods of creativity and repertoire building taken from the work of bell hooks and Cornell West and personal dimensions of knowledge, tacit knowledge and reflective practice. Each program can be viewed in its entirety at www.theculturalworker.com. The first program assembled approximately three hundred people at the Thirty-First Street Baptist Church in Richmond, Virginia. The second convened approximately two hundred people at the Richmond Children's Museum and focused on older foster care youth transitioning from the care of the Richmond Department of Social Services to adulthood. The project examines cultural work as using collective history in the case of the African American Church environment(s) or creating a discursive community event in the case of the foster care youth transition to nurture free spaces that can empower members of a community. Interview responses from two focus groups representing each program's attendees (six persons each) provides information about the effectiveness of the programs, as cultural work, to renew or initiate free space in a discursive community with consequences for empowerment. Through reflective practice and the focus group assessment, the study suggests principles of effective cultural work.

Unfortunately, we too often elevate things to the level of people and downgrade people to the level of things. Jewish philosopher Martin Buber discerns two kinds of relationships—"I-it," which facilitates estrangement, and "I-thou," which facilitates reconciliation. "The Principles of a Cultural Worker"emerge from the research and assert an intentional way toward empowerment and reconciliation while circumventing dysfunction. They form a scaffold to be studied, mastered, and practiced so that individuals, groups, communities, and organizations might "germinate, grow, and reach fulfillment."

Chapter 1: Introduction

...Why don't you write [the] story of this young man... squeezing drop by drop the slave out of himself and waking one fine morning feeling that real human blood, not a slave's, is flowing in his veins.

—Anton Chekov

A linear history will lead us to a linear politics [or vision] and neither will serve us well in an asymmetrical world.

—Elsa Barkley Brown

A cultural worker explores renewing the role of free spaces in discursive communities that empower people and initiating free spaces in new communities. This creative project entailed creating free spaces through the conception, design, and production of two public programs under the topic Walk into Your Season: Cultural Work, Discursive Communities, and Empowerment. These presentations operationalized the role of the cultural worker, explored cultural work, and attempted the renewal or initiation of free spaces of empowerment in two discursive communities. Cultural work unites a group's words, narrative(s), images, visual art, music, film, and other cultural legacies of voice in an effort to inform and inspire individual and collective transformation. It creates a repertoire that exposes empowering features of the group's free spaces.

Walk into Your Season begins by pondering whether a cultural worker can renew the role of free spaces of empowerment to address power differentials utilizing key contributors such as the

1

traditions and language of a culture; the cultural worker's potential to facilitate action and transformation; and the intentional effort to make the hidden transcript of resistance public. As the cultural worker I conceived and facilitated two public programs endeavoring to help groups hold on to and take pride in cultural traditions by contextualizing historical relevance and reenergizing significant stories that reveal a culture's empowering legacy.

Walk into Your Season achieved three primary objectives. The first is that free spaces operationalized the role of the cultural worker in two distinct communities. This involved creating a cultural repertoire through the construction, augmentation, creativity, language, narrative, poetry, music, and tools of the cultures. The second objective was to explore cultural work in two settings using tacit knowing, reflective practice, and creativity, that is, the artistic, tacit, intuitive processes that practitioners bring to situations of problem solving. The third objective of Walk into Your Season was assessing the renewal and initiation of empowerment using focus group responses and reflective practice to (a) ascertain whether participants gained a sense of the history that preceded them and (b) whether they had joined with others or acted on their own to provide better opportunities for their group or themselves.

Walk into Your Season is an art form that reveals elements of free space. By illustrating how free spaces are effective in discursive communities affected by the aftermath of historical dominance and still vulnerable to the ploys of power, Walk into Your Season uses the black church as an institution as exemplified through Thirty-First Street Baptist Church, and older youth transitioning from foster care in the Richmond Department of Social Services to reveal the art form. In other words, *Walk into Your Season* illustrates cultural work in two different settings, one with and one without a history of free spaces. A set of principles for effective cultural work emerges from the study.

Cultural Work

Constructing the concept of cultural work in Walk into Your Season and operationalizing the role of the cultural worker is informed by the work of others. For example, the literary genre highlights the artist efficacy in using language (words, visual art, music, and film) to transform the self and change society (Stauffer 2006, xii). The example of the literary artist as depicted by Zoe Trodd (2006) informs three tasks central to cultural work. The cultural work of *Walk into Your Season* reflects (1) the cultural worker's conveyance and connection of the history, literature, and language of a culture, setting or movement; (2) the cultural worker's potential to facilitate individual and collective understanding (and sometimes renewal) through empathy, shock, and action; and (3) the cultural worker's use of connection, form, appropriation, and collective memory that facilitates action. I will elaborate on the three tasks.

First, the cultural worker strives to know and intentionally convey a group's history, literature, and language (Stauffer 2006). Whether this is attempted through empathy, shock, action or a combination, the availed depth and breadth of the exercise is telling. For example, Trodd (2006) believes that an artist has the ability to use rhetorical skills like empathy and shock to convert audiences and that this ability stretches beyond mere entertainment. Empathy is the ingredient that helps us to feel a victim's pain. The very act of trying to identify with another self and enter his or her thoughts stimulates humanitarian feelings and actions (Burke 1941). Such was the case when Jewish teacher Abel Meeropol published a poem under the pen name Lewis Allen expressing the horror of a lynching. The poem evolved into the song lyrics "Strange Fruit," popularized by singer Billie Holiday. The concerted use of lyrics, music, and voice to elicit sentiment at once swings a punch and rings a moral alarm. Hearing the voice of Billie Holiday singing "Strange Fruit" and seeing the visual of a human body dangling from a southern tree in the

Walk into Your Season Thirty-First Street program audiovisual still elicits empathy through the powerful intersection of vehicles (voice, image, and song). Shock value picks up where empathy leaves off, inspiring us to correct social ills. Remembering human *southern fruit* on the poplar trees illuminates the necessity for power with a purpose in seeking and implementing justice and social change; yet mitigating the polarity that can stymie justice and change is just as necessary.

Second, the cultural worker has the potential to facilitate individual and collective understanding (and sometimes transformation) through empathy, shock, and action (Trodd 2006). Stauffer (2006) parallels the religious revivals described in *Revivals, Awakenings, and Converts* (McLoughin 1978) with the protest artist literature. Each case illustrates the use of empathy, shock, and action. The converted move from states of anxiety and inhibition to states of functionally constructive personal social action" (McLoughlin, 8). This personal action contributes to understanding why revivals are said to change or alter individual lives. Awakenings (those emergent periods of cultural revitalization lasting a generation or more appearing during times of cultural confusion and social stress) can also alter or affect change at the collective or cultural level. There have been relatively few periods of cultural revitalization in America. Most historians attest and allude to just four awakenings (Stauffer, xv): the first three led to the American Revolution, the Civil War, and American entry into World War I, respectively, while the civil rights movement and the Vietnam War were central catalysts to a fourth. These were "jarring disjunctions" in norms, behaviors, and attitudes resulting in societal restructurings (Stauffer 2006) with collective and individual outcomes. Cultural work operates on the belief that the collective is inextricably linked to individual transformation and conversely within each individual rests the first steps toward broader transformation. Even if the cultural worker does not achieve an awakening in the broad collective sense, an individual outcome is produced that can convert negativity, that is, can serve as "an antidote for shame, passivity, and submissiveness" (Stauffer 2006, xvi). Of course cultural work, language, and individual transmutation do not produce instantaneous change. In other words, language does not transform the masses or change everything all at once. Patience and ongoing effort are prerequisites for change and prerequisites for the cultural worker.

Third, cultural work is action that goes beyond empathy and shock, inviting dialogue, debate, and interpretation. However empathy, shock, and language expressed still do not lead directly to action induced social change, just as prophets and preachers cannot eradicate complex mass social problems through the sheer power of their preaching and evangelizing alone. Cultural work is informed by the tools found on the protest artist palette, such as (a) the politics of connection, (b) form, and (c) appropriation (Trodd 2006). These tools are significant in operationalizing the cultural worker and the work of renewing and initiating resources in time and space in the Walk into Your Season public programs. For example, the politics of connection looks at learning from as well as building alliances and meaning across movements. Cultural workers invite people to join, take part, and become empowered in a community. John Steinbeck says, "We spend most of our life trying to be less lonesome ... One of our ancient methods is to tell a story begging the listener to say—and to feel—'Yes, that's the way it is, or at least that's the way I feel it" (Steinbeck 1976, 183). However, it is not only telling the story; it is the form (the repertoire) the cultural worker uses to convey the story that establishes efficacy of the form and its ability to facilitate action. Audience "'commitment' ... reveals itself in how the artist reconstructs the artistic forms at his [or her] disposal, turning authors, readers, and spectators into collaborators" (Eagleton 1976, 12). The cultural worker's skillful use of tools suggests that the master's tools can be appropriated, yet the master's

5

house (subversive and hurtful practices) exposed and ultimately dismantled (Lorde 1984). For example, antilynching protest writers confiscated the rhetoric and imagery of Christianity lynch mobs. Writers like Langston Hughes and W. E. B. Du Bois met white supremacists in their own performance space by "creating figures of black Christs" (Trodd 2006, xxv).

I quote Anton Chekov and Elsa Barkley at the beginning of this chapter. Each inspired my thinking on cultural work and free spaces. Chekov was the muse who prompted me to ponder how people let go of troubling histories, yet maintain the liberation embedded in these histories. How (and where) do people individually and collectively come to reframe bondages that enslave and dominant forces that disempower into counter narratives to free themselves? Elsa Barkley Brown stimulated my thoughts on the individual and collective benefits of building and presenting a creative repertoire that captures the empowering properties of free space.

Brown says "There is a lot that those who are just confronting the necessity to be aware of differences can learn from those who have had to always be aware of such" (Brown 1992, 9). Central to *Walk into Your Season* is the premise that a cultural worker can manifest and facilitate creative mechanisms that engage communal discourse and reframe vexing (sometimes troubling) histories. Toward this goal, as the cultural worker I attempt to create liberating spaces that position, consider, and rely on the past as a counter narrative resource in asserting collective and individual vehicles of empowerment. In this respect the study is at once an effort to specify and define as well as demonstrate the concept of the cultural worker. Using multiple creative avenues (audiovisual, music, story, verse, spoken word) the Walk into Your Season public programs reflect cultural work through some of the collective and individual experiences manifested and exacerbated by historical inequities, power differentials, narrow thinking, faulty logic, and cultural unawareness.

Free Space, Discursive Communities, and Empowerment

As political theorists, historians, and sociologists examined the conditions that foster democratic movements, the notion of free space emerged. Historian E. P. Thompson (1963) never used the term free space per se. Yet he laid the ground work for the free space concept in his seminal work *The Making of The English Working Class*. Thompson created a new kind of history that refused to treat working people as backward, powerless or passive. According to Thompson, class consciousness evolved in the social spaces that people owned in some respects outside the scrutiny and surveillance of their employers such as the taverns and so forth. James Scott (1990) says that the significance of the tavern Thompson identifies as a site of counter-hegemonic discourse comes neither from the drinking it fostered nor the relative insulation from surveillance it provided. Rather, it comes about because the tavern and its nearest equivalent the market (though larger and more anonymous) was the main point of unauthorized assembly for lower class neighbors and workers (Scott 1990). The gathering resembled a neighborhood meeting of subordinates. Privilege was suspended and conversation was encouraged in an atmosphere that excluded hierarchy (121).

Implicit in the conceptualization of free space is the notion that in an ideal democracy, free spaces would serve as vessels of change as well as training arenas for civic leadership and collective problem solving. However, no such ideal society exists. For example, though admittedly referring to the notion of public and hidden transcripts, James Scott (1990) portrays a gap between reality and the ideal which is useful in understanding free space. Scott portrays the public transcript as the self-portrait of dominant elites as they would have themselves seen. However, this depiction is generally lopsided given the usual power of dominant elites to prevail over the performances of others (18). The public transcript conforms closely with the way dominant groups wish to have things appear. It is systematically skewed in the direction of the libretto, the discourse, represented by the dominant (4). On the other hand, the hidden transcript is produced by a different audience and under different constraints of power than the public transcript (5). It takes place "offstage," beyond direct scrutiny by power holders, and is thus derivative in the sense that it includes the offstage speeches, gestures, and practices that contradict, confirm, or inflect what appears in the public transcript (4).

By assessing the discrepancy between the public transcript and the hidden transcript the impact of domination on public discourse can be judged (Scott 1990, 5). Peter Stallybrass and Allon White (1986) surveyed the class cultures that developed from the European taverns, to the middleclass coffee houses, to the church, to the drawing rooms of elite mansions. Stallybrass and White conclude,

> Patterns of discourse are regulated through the forms of corporate assembly in which they are produced ... Discursive space is never completely independent of social place and the formation of new kinds of speech that can be traced through the emergence of new public sites of discourse and the transformation of old ones ... so, in large part, the history of political struggle has been the history of the attempts to control significant sites of assembly and spaces of discourse. (80)

This survey is instructive in regard to the hidden transcript and pivotal in gleaning features of the hidden transcript that inform the notion of free space. The social sites of the hidden transcript are those locations where the unspoken riposte, bridled anger, and tongues harnessed due to dominant relations find unrestrained expression (Scott 1990, 120). It follows that the hidden transcript will be least inhibited under two conditions: first, when it is articulated in a social site where it is least privy to the control, surveillance, and repression of the dominant; and second when the sequestered milieu is composed of close confidants who share similar experiences of domination (120). In this way free spaces create new political identities and capacities but at the same time, illuminate, identify, and underscore gaps between reality and the ideal. As a result new waves of democratic insurgency are created (Evans 2010).

Two questions arise. Does this insurgency suggest that free spaces potentially reflect and reveal an indigenous discourse that can be especially useful in facilitating self-emancipation, as well as collective and individual empowerment? And can failure to intentionally seek and assert this potential encourage the perpetuation of hegemonic themes that marginalize certain groups and ripen conditions for oppression and dysfunction? Organizing conversations emerging from Poland's working class prior to the 1956 riots offer insight on free space because "space was not a gift; it had to be created by people who fought to create it" says Lawrence Goodwin (as cited in Scott 1990, 123). In this way free spaces are dependent on active human agents who create them (Scott 1990, 123).

Historian Howard Zinn illustrates the significance of free space and the efforts of such agents. Zinn exhumes that which is often considered extraneous or peripheral to history—historical bypasses or debris; his modus operandi includes the crannies, pauses, and juxtapositions that constitute cultural life and thus major historical arteries. It is a way of representing the world through the whole collage of entities (Taussig 1986). By taking what Sandra Harding describes as the experience of "people of color and gays and lesbians and working class people and people of various ethnicities" (Hirsch and Olson 2007, 1) and many others, as a starting point— rather than looking at history from some fixed "foundation" in the traditional sense (Harding 2006)—Zinn's approach produces a stronger objectivity, a more generally useful body of knowledge, and a way beyond the impasse(s) that divide. This approach discerns the inscriptions on the fringes and edges of *official* history in order to include them. The inclusion expands understanding of those castigated or marginalized to the role the "other."

In this way, Zinn also accomplishes something else. Through his approach to history Zinn makes hidden transcripts public. He is an exemplification that the cultural worker needs not necessarily be an indigenous member of the culture they work to understand and edify. Zinn (2005) explains,

> I prefer to try to tell the story of the discovery of America from the viewpoint of the Arawaks, of the Constitution from the standpoint of the slaves, of Andrew Jackson as seen by the Cherokees, of the Civil War as seen by the New York Irish ... of the rise of industrialism as seen by young women in the Lowell textile mills, of the Spanish American War as seen by the Cubans, the conquest of the Philippines as seen by black soldiers on Luzon, the Gilded Age as seen by southern farmers, The First World War as seen by the socialists, the Second World War as seen by pacifists, the New Deal as seen by blacks in Harlem, the postwar American empire as seen through peons in Latin America. And so on, to the limited extent that any one person, however he or she strains, can 'see' history from the stand point of others. My point is not to grieve for the victims and denounce the executioners ... In the short run (and so far, human history has consisted only of short runs), the victims, themselves desperate and tainted with the culture that oppresses them, turn on the other victims. (10)

Walk into Your Season strives to see the discursive community from the standpoint of its community members. The cultural work of *Walk into Your Season* is predicated on building a creative repertoire that exposes empowering features of free space. Cultural work as repertoire building and creating free space is central to democratic progress and important due to its work in (a) identifying, engaging, and illuminating, the empowering features of free space (b) discerning the gaps between reality and the democratic ideal, (c) facilitating a creative space in which recognized gaps can be explored, (d) building a repertoire that empowers individually and collectively through renewal and initiation, (e) making hidden transcripts public when appropriate, and (f) celebrating the emergent creative repertoire in the community.

The African American Church as a Free Space

Historically, in the black experience the quest for recognition and validation in most instances occurred on the cultural, social, and ideological turf of Caucasian people. Rules were made outside and beyond the control of most African Americans. The black church, therefore, is unique in American culture. The term black church is a shorthand rubric that refers to denominationally diverse black Christian communities that came into being when African American slaves decided (often at great peril) to choose Jesus and share with one another their common Christian sense of purpose and Christian understanding of their circumstances (West 1999c, 426). Preoccupation with the "good news" proclaimed by Jesus of Nazareth is steeped in the unique African American encounter with the modern world conceptualized by the existential (being-in-the-world yet resisting dread and despair). As such, the black church remained the most important institution in the black community, beholden only to its members. Congregants may have led a marginal existence shaped by dominance in society, but their churches were counter publics; communities where marginal boundaries did not exist. Their churches were arenas where they were free to gather and enact weekly through ritual and song their shared heritage (Evans 2010). Singing, poetry, rhythms, sermons, pooling their food and resources, and discussions of their conditions and heritage were a part of their communal experience.

This communal experience contained two organic intellectual traditions in African American heritage: the black Christian tradition of preaching and the black musical tradition of performance (West 1991). These traditions are indigenous to African American life and the intellectual due to achieving creative progress through reflection and development. Both (the sermonic and the music) were pivotal in advancing the civil rights movement. Both says West though linked to the mind, are improvisational, oral, and dramatic (136). However, these traditions have "institutional matrices over time and space within which there are accepted rules of procedure, criteria for judgment, canons for assessing performance, models of past achievement and present emulation, and an acknowledged succession and accumulation of superb accomplishments" (136). Both are rooted in black life and possess what literate forms of black intellectual activity lack—strong institutional channels to sustain traditions. It is not that great literate intellectuals have not existed. Ralph Ellison, James Baldwin, W. E. B. Dubois, Zora Neale Hurston, and Toni Morrison are examples of their existence. However, so far as institutional channels to sustain traditions over time, only the church provided such a vehicle.

Independent Living As a Discursive Community

Understanding the historical role of the black church as an institution is germane to capturing edifying opportunities intrinsic to free spaces. Similarly, understanding the historical arc of diverse groups is central to seizing intrinsic opportunities. Historically African Americans had to submit to the dominant culture and could not readily express their own concerns, desires, heritage, and needs. They could not share and reflect on mutual concerns to develop creative solutions to their problems in the larger society. However in the black church African Americans found a space to express and affirm their beliefs, articulate their vulnerabilities, and become empowered.

The problem of moving from slavery and racial subordination has a parallel to transitioning from foster care. In order to understand the needs of youth transitioning from foster care it is important to be aware of the historical roots and trajectory of oppressive disempowering practices that necessitate the independent living (IL) program. Revisiting the travail of Willie Palmer facilitates an understanding regarding the challenges at the root of the IL program's inception. Palmer was emancipated from foster care in 1985 from the State of New York. He was eighteen years old and left foster care homeless, unemployed, and allegedly possessing only a plastic bag with his belongings. The financial safety net, marketable skills, and family and community network most young people need to thrive and survive were nonexistent in Palmer's life.

Palmer's plight is now legendary. He sued the state of New York, in the case *Palmer v. Cuomo*, won the case, and the independent living initiative was born. Palmer's unfortunate circumstance served as the catalyst for a cause that continues to gain national attention. Ultimately his efforts along with those of others like him manifested the Foster Care Independence Act of 1999 and the John H. Chafee Foster Care Independence Program, signed by President William Clinton in December 1999. This law provides expanded funding to states and mandates that they provide more support, services, training and life skills education to youth in foster care and their caregivers.[1]

The Walk into Your Season social work event is an effort to explain independent living as a free space and discursive community to a social work audience. The necessity of doing so resides in creating environments that nurture opportunities for community building, healing, identity and cultural transmission, wisdom transmission,

---

1 National Independent Living Association on Willie Palmer retrieved from http://www.nilausa.org/windowhistory.htm and Pennsylvania Child Welfare Training Program Power Point on Willie Palmer, Foster Care Independence Act of 1999, and Independent Living retrieved from http://www.pacwcbt.pitt.edu/curriculum/202%20Foundations%20of%20IL%20Overview/handouts/Resource_Guide%5B1%5D.pdf.

and social capital. Making a commitment to squeeze out the blood of victimization, even if drop by drop through attempts such as Walk into Your Season, is the liberation Chekov captures in his statement. Casting a net that envelops the whole story is the truth serum Elsa Barkley Brown offers. She does so through the wide lens depth and breadth of history that can empower both venerable and emergent communities rather than restrict them. As the cultural worker, I used familiar genres (music, stories, audiovisuals, participants, and so on) in an attempt to create a free space in an evolving discursive community. This was cultural work using the knowledge of a new community and many of the genres found empowering in an established community to demonstrate the opportunities of free space.

Succinctly, the IL event is conceived as an opportunity to create a free space. This is attempted through the foster care community, specifically independent living. Anchored upon the example of the historical role of the black church as an institution through the lens of the Thirty-First Street community, the Walk into your Season program concept revisits the historical role of free spaces to empower people and considers their initiation in new settings, such as social services, by a cultural worker. *Walk into Your Season: The Art of Cultural Work* is the emergent traveling companion that retraces the conceptual journey and its manifold relevance.

Chapter 2: Cultural Work, Free Space, and Empowerment

Our whole mode of thinking must be turned upside down ... A political being is not to be defined as the citizen he has been, as an abstract, disconnected bearer of rights, privileges, and immunities, but as a person whose existence is located in a particular place and draws its sustenance from circumscribed relationships, family, friends, church, neighborhood, workplace, community, town, city.

—Sheldon Wolin

Power ... is the ability to achieve purpose. It is the strength required to bring about social, political, or economic changes. In this sense power is not only desirable but necessary in order to implement the demands of love and justice. One of the greatest problems of history is that concepts of love and power are usually contrasted as polar opposites. Love is identified as a resignation of power and power with a denial of love ... what is needed is a realization that power without love is reckless and abusive and that love without power is sentimental and anemic.

—Martin Luther King Jr.

This chapter describes the cultural worker in relationship to the central concerns of cultural work, free space, discursive communities, and empowerment. I use the knowledge presented in this chapter to illustrate and advance these factors in renewing and creating the free spaces of Walk into Your Season. Creativity, cultural work, and reflective practice are presented and described in this chapter as concepts that inform the study. It is much easier to simply simulate abstractions on paper than it is to create a vessel that illustrates these abstractions in real time and then witness and document the experience. The bottom up audacity Sheldon Wolin articulates fortifies my resolve to make the abstract observable in Walk into Your Season by actually creating a laboratory that demonstrates his words—a vehicle that demonstrates the *sustenance drawn from circumscribed relationships, family, friends, church, neighborhood, workplace, community, town, and city,* thus exposing the opportunities therein. Alongside identifying and convening these relationships and communities I first had to envision the entities embedded in them—cultural work and the strivings of the cultural worker.

Culture and the Cultural Worker

Drawing from Stauffer (2006), in the broadest sense cultural work uses language (words, visual art, music, film, and voice) to inform and inspire individuals and communities to transform themselves. Cultural work combines "voice, knowledge, intelligence, and experience of a story [conscious] leader [facilitator, scholar-artist], to unite a group of people" (Gilliam 2006, v) with a goal of embracing or creating a space that empowers. Examples abound of individuals who activate voice, language, and experience or who invoke counter narratives to inspire others to action (Carson 2001; Chapman 1972; Douglas circa 1864; Moody 1968). An individual committing to cultural work as conceived in this study can function as a catalyst, guide, mirror, and facilitator of social change, seeking implicit and explicit solutions to collective and individual problems.

If the cultural worker uses voice, knowledge, intelligence, and story to unite people with a goal of embracing or creating a space that empowers, what is culture? How is it defined? Why is this cultural worker central to it? George Kelly (1955) relates culture as the shared constructions of experience made possible because people belonging to a given group are similar in what they expect from one another and hold similar perceptions of what is expected of them. Kelly (1995, 695–696) held that ethnicity, church membership, race, nationality, social class, and language groups demonstrate affiliations with similar constructions of experience. A repertoire of relevant perceptual experiences is cultivated in each type of group to which a person is affiliated (697).

Kelly's definition is insightful, yet it is in some respects incomplete. It does not account for dissimilarity in expectations amongst members of the same cultural group and does not make a distinction between group unity and shared identity. The definition does not reveal the depth (that is, the historical impact) and the breadth (the implicit and explicit behavioral considerations) of culture.

Admittedly, it is difficult to do so in any single definition. Still the lapse is nonetheless troublesome. Kelly's definition is misleading since it implies that all people holding church membership or all young people or all middleclass people cultivate the same repertoire of perceptual experiences in these generalized groups. If the conception is not dangerous, it is certainly insufficient. It portends hegemony and suggest that there is only one discourse—one narrative in these groups. Kelly's definition is a rendering out of sync with what Alvin Gouldner (1979) depicts as creating a culture of critical and careful discourse. Members of the same group often cultivate disparate experiences due to different needs, interests, and histories. For instance, the cultural legacy of the black church as an institution may be different from that of its counterpart in another community. The cultural resources of youth transitioning from foster care may be very different from those of a youth who has never been estranged from his or her parents.

Fortunately, by critically reviewing concepts and definitions, Alfred Kroeber and Clyde Kluckhohn (1952) synthesized more than one hundred definitions of culture. They arrived at a comprehensive definition that gained and maintains wide acceptance:

> Culture consists of patterns, explicit and implicit, of and for behavior acquired and transmitted by symbols, constituting the distinctive achievement of human groups ... The essential core of culture consists of traditional (i.e., historical derived and selected) ideas and especially their attached values; culture systems may, on the one hand, be considered as products of action, on the other, as conditioning elements of future action. (Kroeber and Kluckhohn in Adler 2008, 18)

Nancy Adler (2008) reaffirms Kroeber and Kluckhohn's definition. Culture is viewed as (a) something shared by most members of a given social group, (b) something older group members pass on to younger group members, and (c) something that structures one's perception of the world or shapes behavior (as in the case of morals, customs, and laws).

A cultural worker is conscious of the interplay among the disparity of cultural definitions and their elements—for example, the shared constructions and repertoire of experiences Kelly outlines; the transmittal of explicit and implicit patterns that Kroeber and Kluckhohn articulate; and the collective sharing and intergenerational renewal Adler confirms.

The Cultural Worker

The notion of the cultural worker finds context in the work of philosopher Michel Foucault (1984b) and scholar/writer Cornel West (1999b). Foucault's investigation concentrates on the emergence of what at that time was a new paradigm in the connection between theory and practice. Foucault examines the relational complexities surrounding the discursive ways in which and the institutional means through which regimes of truth ('general politics of truth') come about. That is, "the types of discourse [a society] accepts and makes function as true" (Foucault 1984b, 73) are constituted over time and space. According to West (1999b) this results in a new conception of the intellectual as artist, and critic (119). West describes this new conception as the cultural worker; one who is open to others (including the mainstream) yet focused and grounded in affirming and enabling subcultures of criticism. This is a person who also accepts the intellectual challenge of analyzing the world for the purpose of changing it (Cone 1986). It is a notion that supports Gouldner's (1979) conception regarding creating a culture of critical and careful discourse.

Michel Foucault (1984) brings understanding to the concept of cultural worker by making a distinction between the "universal intellectual" and the "specific intellectual." Foucault describes the specific intellectual in the political sense as one who "utilizes his [or her] knowledge, his [or her] competence, and his [or her] relation to truth in the field of political struggles" (70). Foucault portrays the universal intellectual as the writer who once served as a spokesperson for universal consciousness. However, when specific activity began to serve as a basis for politicization, social workers, teachers, laboratory technicians, magistrates, doctors, sociologists, and so on became able to participate within their own fields as well as through mutual exchange and support. This in large measure facilitates the intellectual's interaction with everyday problems specific to the struggles, challenges, and problems of everyday people, establishing the "specific" intellectual (Foucault 1984). Through the specific intellectual's involvement with these specific sectors (again, the family, the hospital, the university, the church), the intellectual gains an immediate and concrete awareness of struggles, challenges, and problems endemic and specific to everyday life and problems germane to the mainstream, middle- and low-income people, and marginalized people.

Even in instances where the specific intellectual's struggle(s) may be different from those of everyday people, Foucault (1984b) says that the specific intellectual's awareness, interaction, and involvement in these struggles brings the intellectual closer to the everyday experiences of everyday people (the mainstream). Foucault attributes this to (a) the intellectual's interfacing with real, everyday struggles and challenges, and (b) the intellectual's confrontations with similar adversaries albeit in different forms (68–70). This notion is akin to a conception of the person closest to the work, doing the work.

This interaction suggests the emergence not only of the "specific" intellectual, but perhaps a configuration that allows the rearticulation of areas once separated. This paradigm shift facilitates lateral connections across different forms of knowledge (Foucault 1984b). The rearticulation confronts the hierarchical separation of professions and the resultant resistance to practitioner interaction embedded in the traditional Technical Rationality approach (Schön 1983). When asked what prompted this paradigm shift marking the emergence of this specific intellectual, Foucault said that in his view the "specific" intellectual came after World War II:

> Perhaps it was the atomic scientist [Oppenheimer] who acted as the point of transition between the universal and the specific intellectual. It's because he had a direct and localized relation to scientific knowledge and institutions that the atomic scientist could make his intervention; but since the nuclear threat affected the whole human race and the fate of the world, his discourse could at the same time be the discourse of the universal. Under the rubric of this protest, which concerned the entire world, the atomic expert brought into play his specific position in the order of knowledge. (1984b, 69)

Foucault's conception establishes an intellectual who reaches into the family, the hospital, the university, and the church at the precise (hence specific) juncture where his or her conditions of work or life situate them (Foucault 1984b). The conception of the specific intellectual informs the role of the cultural worker.

Free Space and the Discursive Community

Like E. P. Thompson, Jurgen Habermas (1991) also never used the term free space per se, yet enhances the concept through his theoretical inquiries into public life. The political public sphere Habermas describes represents private people who come together as a public to use their reason critically. He also relates this public sphere as a discursive space where people and groups gather to discuss mutual concerns and common interests and to reach common judgment. Rather than simply a place, it is a series of actions. And because they quickly evolve into schools for public engagement and political action, these spaces become freedom arenas. Two things make a free space free. First, it is their ability to escape surveillance so that they authentically and truly belong to the people who create and use them. Second, the degree to which they function as "publics" where difference does not create hierarchy (Evans 2010, 360). Habermas in effect considers the public sphere as a *space* where discussions on matters of mutual interest can emerge. Ordinary people can "discover themselves as civic actors" (Evans 2010, 360). People without power who are lacking skills of public life (analyzing power, public speaking, strategic thinking, listening to alternate viewpoints and so on) can gain them in free space.

Sara Evans (2010) considers how it comes about that people who are not in the seat of power are able to develop a shared identity (a "we"), so as to venture from a sense of powerlessness intrinsic to victimhood to a sense that their world should and could change? German sociologist Ferdinand Tönnies (1926) informs the meaning of this shared identity. Tönnies established a distinction between society (*Gesellschaft*) and community (*Gemeinschaft*).

While *Gesellschaft* (often translated as society or civil society) relates to the conscious choices of relatively independent individuals, *Gemeinschaft* is a subjective community of inner relations. As such, community relies on "the consciousness of belonging together and the affirmation of the condition of mutual dependence which is posed by that affirmation" (Tönnies 1926, 69). In this respect the implication is that a closeness exists (though not rigidly), says sociologist Craig Calhoun (1980), so far as face to face contact, commonality of purpose, familiarity, and dependability (111).

The terms "social space" and "lived space" address the daily, lived character of relationships and networks, many of which formed the basis of social movements. The concept evolves from traditions of phenomenology, ethnology, and social geography and addresses the ways places are connected and organized (an objective physical dimension) as well as how we perceive and understand space as a familiar, customary part of daily experience (the subjective dimension) (Evans and Boyte 1986). They are particular settings, spaces or environments in the community in which people can "learn a new self-respect, a deeper and more assertive group identity, public skills, and values of cooperation and civic virtue" (17).

The potential exists in these environments for spaces to evolve that create and nurture opportunities for community building, healing, identity and cultural transmission, wisdom transmission, social capital, and psychosymbolic and psychopolitical empowerment (Boyte 1984; Evans 2010; Evans and Boyte 1986; Couto 1999). The relevance of these spaces rests in the inability for some people in subjugated positions and groups to achieve these attributes in the larger society because of their marginal location. However, while marginalized and disempowered in the larger society, they become empowered in free spaces. Habermas informs contemporary understanding of these "publics" as free spaces where status is irrelevant. In other words "publics" can be described as the public sphere where discussion replaces the "celebration of rank with a tact befitting equals" (1991, 36). Habermas critic Nancy Fraser (1990) enriches the discussion of free spaces by conceptualizing the emergence of "counterpublics," marginal groups excluded from elite domination of public life. As such, free spaces are repositories for counter cultural understandings that represent the alternative and critical experience of face-to-face movements, organizations, and communities

Free spaces as social spaces can vary in their effectiveness (Evans 2010). They can manifest as static and dynamic or enduring and transient. Nevertheless, movements that are deeply democratic create spaces or environments where people can change and grow as they begin to act. The experimentation, rethinking, and learning that is allowed in the space facilitates participants discovering themselves and new democratic potentials within themselves (Evans 2010). Ordinary, innovative, and visionary narratives emerge (Gardner and Laskin 1995). Meanwhile, ordinary narratives unveil hidden dimensions of power, innovative, and visionary narratives reveal and express the extraordinary worth of a subordinate group, possibility of new configurations, and the unjust falsehood of power (Couto 1993).

These narratives have audiences that give them power. Innovative and visionary narratives start out with small audiences before winning over larger audiences that give them legitimacy as a counter narrative. For example, the narratives of the abolition of slavery expanded equality of women. The rights of the disabled moved from visionary and innovative backstage narratives, away from ordinary narratives of neglect or repression, into free spaces with appreciative (though smaller) audiences (Couto 2007). Also, the notion of difference must be considered in relationship to space. Those considered different by the dominant culture need and benefit from free spaces that confront hegemonic themes.

Free spaces are also a reminder that class consciousness evolved in social spaces in which working people held ownership in some sense (Thompson 1963). Evans explains that "no human community matches an idealized definition yet the concept of free spaces has revealing explanatory power because it makes sense of activism that otherwise might seem to come out of nowhere and it greatly enriches our understanding of the dynamics of democracy" (2010, 361). Entities can become free spaces where the democratic threads of tradition can be nourished in the heart of hierarchy (360). In the instance of African Americans, for example, since emancipation, the *black church* was one of the few institutions under the jurisdiction of local African Americans. The church as a free space illustrates an attempt to embrace culture and maintain historical connection. It was (and debatably still is) an example of what Molefi Kete Asante (1987) describes as an Afrocentric perspective.

Asante considers both Afrocentricsm and Eurocentrism as equally valid cultural traditions. He does not esteem one over the other. However, while Eurocentricsm expresses an Anglo-European civilization and is characterized as dualistic, materialistic, and linear, by contrast Afrocentrism places African experience at the center of its worldview. Asante (1987) looks at Afrocentricsm as an alternative paradigm of social knowledge, considering it a critique of the social sciences. He believes it employs a holistic approach to knowledge and society, placing value on harmony, spirituality, and unity. He assumes that despite the diversity of African cultures there is a core African identity apparent not only in Africa but in the African Diaspora.

On the other hand Anthony Appiah (1992) is skeptical, saying that whatever Africans share, common language, common traditional culture, common conceptual vocabulary or religion are nonexistent and that in fact "we do not even belong to a common race" (26). Yet it is of particular interest that Appiah does not totally relinquish the idea of common identity, conceding that invoking African identity is useful in bringing about political identity. African unity remains compelling culturally and politically partially because of commonalities in African history and social struggles. Consequently Appiah defends the appeal to African identity absent of strong (and what he terms misleading) claims to unity.

Appiah and Asante are just two voices within the breadth and depth of these historical discourses on race and identity. I point to them however because I believe that though their viewpoints contrast in many respects, they shed light on how a hidden transcript was made public and what that means today. Negritude, once stigmatized (like the term black regarding ethnicity in the United States), was turned into a point of pride (Asante 1987). Such identity transformation is contingent upon the free social spaces that affirmed not only the right, but also the necessity for blacks to enter the global community as equals, and to acquire and maintain "intrapsychic defenses" (group solidarity, pride, and traditions) while in pursuit of and as a result of political identity (Evans and Boyte 1986, 28).

Considering all these factors, how then do people develop new visions where elements of tradition do not become justifications for continued retribution, but rather become resources for democratic insurgency (Evans 2010)? Consider civil society. Civil society is the primary location of free space and historically the conception and establishment of free space has resulted in building civil society in places where it was previously weak, vulnerable or nonexistent (Evans 2010). Civil society is discerned in several ways. It has an associational aspect in that it includes the arena of voluntary associations around shared values, purpose, and interests, including community groups, faith based organizations, professional associations, self-help groups, trade unions, and nongovernmental organizations. It is also shorthand for the good society in which people would like to live. Close to "Walk in Your Season" is the concept of civil society as an arena for public deliberations, meaning that it is the public space in which societal differences, social problems, public policy, government action, and matters of community and cultural identity are developed and debated. In short, civil society is a goal (a good society), a means of achieving the goal (associational), and a framework for engaging with one another (spaces of deliberation). Free spaces allow for learning, experimentation, and opportunities for people to discover within themselves new democratic potentials (Naidoo and Bannerjee 2010).

Power and Empowerment

To consider the issue of empowerment in the free space of the discursive community, one must first contemplate and explore the ingredients of power, particularly since the two terms (power and empowerment) are too often inappropriately and mistakenly commingled. Some researchers and leaders incorrectly equate feelings of empowerment with influence over others and with actual power (Perkins 2010). Then too there are levels of power and dimensions seen and unseen. Foucault (1980), for example, makes a distinction between visible and hidden forms of power. Hayward (1998) relies on the concept of boundary put forth by Foucault and others and suggests that power can be understood "as the network of social boundaries that delimit fields of possible action"; whereas freedom, on the other hand, "is the capacity to participate effectively in shaping the social limits that define what is possible" (2).

A conundrum rests in the spread and adoption of the language and discourse of participation and inclusion by powerful actors, who confuse the boundaries of who has authority and who does not; who can be on the "inside" and who is cast on the periphery "outside" of decision and policy making arenas; and how the power dynamics of these arenas actually work (Gaventa and Pettit 2010). Gaventa and Pettit consider how to challenge existing power relations of inequality and exclusion. They posit that leaders and practitioners wanting to shift power relations so as to make them more just, inclusive, equitable, or democratic, must learn and develop capacities to promote participatory and democratic processes. Central to the task is finding ways of surfacing power dynamics and identifying strategies that can shift power in favor of excluded or marginalized groups. This means that leaders, facilitators, and workers must understand more about where and how to engage (Gaventa and Pettit 2010).

To aid in this regard Gaventa and Pettit (2010) searched for approaches that might make the implied power relationship more explicit and at the same time explore the range of configurations regarding spaces and interrelationships. Supported by the work of Steven Lukes, Gaventa and Pettit offer a visual depiction of visible, hidden, and invisible dimensions of power. It is a framework for reflecting upon and analyzing power dimensions. These dimensions are portrayed in the researchers' rubric power cube.

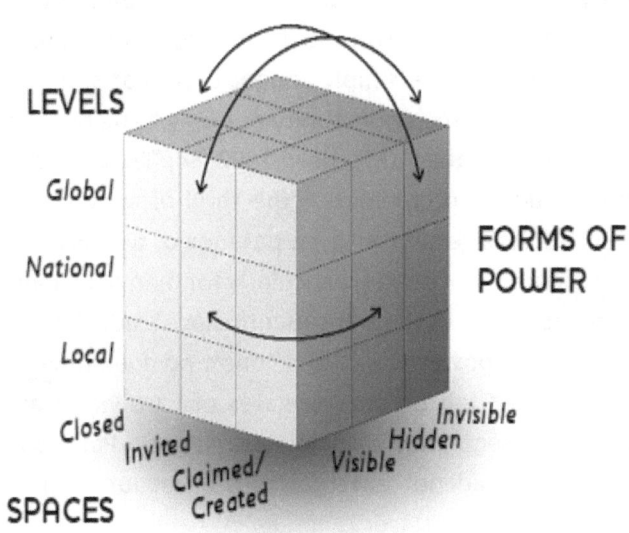

Figure 1   The power cube: Power in spaces and places of participation (Gaventa and Pettit 2010)

Using the power cube, we can assess the possibilities of transformative action in various spaces. Each of these dimensions— the spaces, places, and forms of power—is separate but also interrelated. This tool allows cultural workers and practitioners an opportunity to map the types of power that need to be challenged. This cube also suggests that cultural workers should look at local forms of hidden and invisible power within the discursive community. Succinctly, it is no longer sufficient to call for greater public consultation or citizen participation without understanding how power, in its many forms, can mediate and distort these processes (Gaventa and Pettit 2010).

The construction of blackness and enslavement illustrates the dramatic polarity of skin color, the not-free and the not-me. Contemporary times bear witness to the connection between power, participation, and marginality, but contemporary times are preceded by historical references of dominance. Immigrants sought escape (from social ostracism, prison, poverty, and sometimes death); the clerical scholarly group sought the adventure in founding a colony; and the merchants quite simply sought cash. For some people it was a "once in a lifetime opportunity not only to be born again but born again in new clothes" (Morrison 1992, 34). They could dispense with genuflection and commence the thrill of command that lay waiting ahead. As a result the great paradox of western modernity is that democracy flourished (particularly for men of property) right besides the flowering of the transatlantic slave trade. For Caucasian men of property, power—control of one's own destiny—replaced the powerlessness felt before the gates of European class, caste, and cunning persecution. As sociologist Orlando Patterson (1982) injects, freedom did not emerge from a vacuum. And nothing highlights freedom like slavery.

In that construction of blackness and enslavement that Morrison and Patterson reference emerges the dramatic polarity of skin color, the not-free and the not-me. What arose from the collective need to relieve internal fears and rationalize external exploitation says Toni Morrison (1992) was an American Africanism—a fabricated brew of darkness, otherness, alarm, and desire that is uniquely American. (Morrison uses Africanism in this context as a term for connotative and denotative blackness that African peoples have come to signify and the whole range of views, assumptions, readings, and misreadings that accompany Eurocentric learning about these peoples. This is not the same context as that of philosopher Valentine Mudimbe who uses Africanism to suggest the larger body of knowledge on Africa.) Morrison describes the lived experience of many "others" not as such because they are African American but because they live (for any number of reasons and social locations) this denotative and connotative existence daily.

Audre Lorde (1984) refers to this denotative and connotative existence as marginalization, describing it as the *mythical norm* in which the trappings of power, shaped by certain characteristics (heterosexual, white, financially secure, male, Christian, etc.), which are weighted differently singularly and promoted as a stable center around which everything else must revolve (116). The myth is perpetuated by those it stands to serve and their interests. However, the myth can also be internalized by those oppressed by it. It is a binary frame work describes Barbara Christian (1988) that "sees the rest of the world as minor and tries to convince the rest of the world that it is major, usually through force and then through language, even as it claims many of the ideas that we, its 'historical' other, have known and spoken about for so long. For many of us have never conceived of ourselves only as somebody's other" (70).

Yet black history is a powerful demonstration of the way the oppressed and powerless can reveal and utilize the subversive themes veiled in the dominant culture as resources for struggle, resistance, and self-affirmation (Evans and Boyte 1986). Michel Foucault (1980, 1984a) emerges as a critical voice regarding the denial of dominant prejudices, power webs, and intentionally

29

hidden accounts of history. Earlier discussion presented Foucault's notion as related to culture. But here his conceptions relative to power are considered. This is central to the notion conceived in this study that power is embedded in culture. Among Foucault's most noteworthy: (a) though power can function negatively by repressing or constraining individuals, it also can function positively to create and form individuals themselves ("Do not concentrate the study of the punitive mechanisms on their 'repressive' effects alone … but situate them in a whole series of their possible positive effects" [1984a, 170]); (b) there is a nexus between the growth of knowledge and power ("make the technology of power the very principle both of the humanization of the penal system and of the knowledge of man" [1984a, 171]); and (c) power functions to form and influence individuals through certain technologies (not as in computer technology but as in strategic techniques)—*the microphysics of power* which cannot be possessed through acquisition appropriation but instead is exercised:

Microphysics presupposes that the power exercised on the body is conceived not as a property but as a strategy; that its effects of domination are attributed not to "appropriation" but to dispositions, maneuvers, tactics, techniques, and functionings; that one should decipher it in a network of relations, constantly in tension, in activity, rather than a privilege that one must possess; that one should take as its model a perpetual battle, rather than a contract regulating a transaction or the conquest of a territory. In short this power is exercised rather than possessed; it is not the "privilege," acquired or preserved, of the dominant class but the overall effect of its strategic positions—an effect that is manifested and sometimes extended by the position of those who are dominated (Foucault 1984a, 174).

If power is strategic then empowerment must be intentional. It was not until Barbara Solomon's work was presented in the publication *Black Empowerment: Social Work in Oppressed*

Communities that the term empowerment appeared in its current usage. Here Solomon (1976) recommends an empowerment approach to social work in African American communities. She explains that "theories of practice hold particular dangers when the client is Afro American and experiencing powerlessness from systematic sources" (Solomon 1982, 177). This suggests that to facilitate client empowerment, that which is factual must be reframed and reinvented. Furthermore, workers and clinicians must possess the ability to accurately evaluate emic (culture specific) and etic (universal) hypotheses related to people from identified groups and to develop accurate conceptualizations, including awareness of when clinical issues involve cultural dimensions (APA 1993; AAPA, ABPsi, NLPA, and SIP 2003) and when theoretical orientation needs to be adapted for more effective work with members of identified groups (Hansen et al. 2000).

Solomon (1982) suggests that the verity and saliency of this approach is demonstrated in the case of one fifty-year-old African American man and his experience with two psychodynamically trained therapists. After the death of his wife, [Mr. X] felt powerless, meaningless and depressed. The first therapist centered treatment on earlier relationships to caretakers as they related to feelings about his wife—a western approach. Soon thereafter Mr. X attempted suicide. The second therapist (also psychodynamically trained) expanded the focus of treatment to include Mr. X's experiences with the wider ethno system. It was of particular interest to the therapist that he was college educated but never received any other kind of employment beyond the post office. He worked in that capacity for twenty years. "No one wants you when you're over 50 ... especially if you're black" (177) he stated in one therapy session. Yet he also revealed that he had always dreamed of having his own business. As an adjunct to his regular therapy sessions, Mr. X was referred to a self-help group made up of persons interested in making "mid-life career changes." He remained in therapy and the self-help group until he had successfully negotiated a franchise with a national auto parts store (Solomon 1982).

The second therapist's ability to shift gears drawing from a counseling repertoire that could tune into the client's historical perspective; facilitate a space to reconsider discarded dreams and present needs; and re-member cultural recollections, facilitated an invaluably clear sense of life changing empowerment. It helps the client to "understand the complex interplay between what is experienced intra-psychically and what is experienced outside in the world. Through this understanding [workers] can help the [people] to differentiate between the two and help [them] feel empowered and understood" (Jackson 2000, 8). This is of great benefit in the context of [a person's] feelings of powerlessness and disenfranchisement from systematic resources in the community (Solomon 1982).

In the years that have followed Solomon's pioneering work offering empowerment as an approach to social work in African American communities, policy makers, researchers, prevention specialists, program administrators, and politicians have become interested in the empowerment concept. P. L. Berger and Neuhaus (1977) used the term as a guide for reforming public policy. Rappaport (1981) issued a call for adopting a social policy of empowerment. Still there is remaining work and there are many unanswered questions. Rappaport (1984) explained that "we do not know what empowerment is ... [but] we know it when we see it" (2). To most people, it is a popular but vague word heard in political, community development, management, or therapeutic-wellness circles. Perkins (1995) voices concern that this ambiguity ultimately inhibits the development of theory, scientific understanding, and sound program planning and policy making.

Also, the term empowerment though seemingly omnipresent of late, is not omniscient. Saying *we know it when we see it* does not suffice. *It* cannot be personified without action, reflection and exploration. As Gaventa and Pettit (2010) illustrate through the power cube description, in order to facilitate empowerment, the spaces where power resides (closed, invited, claimed/created), levels of power (global, national, local), and forms in which power exists (visible, hidden, invisible) must be clarified. Locating the space allows the cultural worker to expose the creative features inherent in the space. For example, the Walk into Your Season venues represent a claimed/created space—the black church—and an invited space—the children's museum. This power cube also illustrates the forms of hidden and invisible power within the discursive community that I explore.

Empowerment has been defined as an intentional ongoing process centered in the local community, predicated on mutual respect, caring, critical reflection, and group participation through which people who do not have an equal share of valued resources acquire greater access to and control over those resources. In other words empowerment is described as a process through which people gain control over their lives, democratic participation in the life of their community, and a critical understanding of their environment (Perkins and Zimmerman 1995).

It is a construct that theoretically links mutual help with well-being to create a responsive community. For example, an important meaning making process is developing a sense of self and/or unique purpose and then being able to see oneself as part of the larger whole or environment along with a sense of being able to shape that environment (Gilliam 2006). The commonalities across these definitions are that empowerment (a) is a process; (b) occurs in communities (and organizations); (c) involves active participation, critical reflection, awareness and understanding (i.e., consciousness raising about the influence of powerful political and economic structures and interests); and (d), involves access to and control over important decisions and resources (Perkins 1995).

The importance of visionary, talented, and committed leadership (such as that of a cultural worker) as a setting context for empowerment is supported, for instance, by Evans and Boyte's (1986) historical research into civil rights, feminist, and other democratic social movements. The historical evidence suggests that members of such organizations benefited from their leaders' vision and active role modeling. We should also include creating a climate of mutual respect and caring, which may be especially important for cultural workers to include in their understanding and practice of empowerment (Gutierrez and Ortega 1991).

Empowerment can also be thought of as the life and outlook-changing outcome of such a process for individuals, organizations, and whole communities. Uprisings of disconnected individuals easily succumb to authoritarian, demagogic leaders because (a) people lack the wherewithal to envision a public arena where different perspectives can engage in a process of collective problem solving, and/or (b) they lack the necessary skills to hold such leaders accountable (Evans 2010). Moreover, the challenges faced today by agents of progressive social change—are fraught with complexity and contradiction since they arise from the multiple forms of power that can marginalize and exclude some people while enlarging the voices, recognition, and influence of others (Gaventa and Pettit 2010).

Even so, in free spaces people build networks and discover new political thoughts about the world. Empowerment connects individual competencies and strengths, proactive behaviors and natural healing systems (Rappaport 1981, 1984). Empowerment theories include processes and outcomes, suggesting that structures, actions, and activities may empower and that process outcomes result in a level of being empowered (Swift and Levin 1987). Maton and Salem (1995) view empowerment as a process that enables people through participation with others to achieve their personal goals. This description recognizes individual motivations as well as collective action. As an enabling process this description allows examination of empowering characteristics across a variety of community settings, organizations, and groups without ignoring the diversification of respective needs that arise in discursive communities. Implicit in the description is the creativity of cultural work that facilitates characteristics, outcomes, and processes exemplified in the empowering settings that Maton and Salem (1995) describe. These settings exemplify (a) leadership that is inspiring; (b) a motivating belief system that inspires growth; (c) a meaningful opportunity role structure that is highly accessible and multifunctional; and (d) an impressive array of social supports that is peer based, encompassing, and provides a sense of community (Maton and Salem 1995).

Creativity

The concept of creativity informs *Walk into Your Season* because creativity is central to innovation, which is in turn central to cultural work. Human creativity, a source of fascination and speculation, did not become a focus of rigorous academic study until the 1950s. Since then multiple approaches to creativity have arisen, most of which are rooted in specific academic disciplines (Golden 2010). Major approaches identified to the study of creativity include the mystical, pragmatic, psychodynamic, psychometric, cognitive, social-personality, and confluence approaches (Sternberg and Lubart 1999). This diversity in approach makes for a plethora of definitions. From that multitude a broad definition of creativity incorporating all these concepts and ideas from many current researchers is that creativity is the production of something innovative that has value (Piirto 2004; Puccio et al. 2007). I believe, however, that the creativity of cultural work needs and deserves further and more specific context. In fact, two areas in creativity studies that are currently receiving attention from researchers are group creativity and the interplay between culture and creativity (Golden 2010). This interplay is central to the cultural work that informs *Walk into Your Season*. My rationale for this belief reaches back to the conceptualizations expressed through Foucault's (1984b) specific intellectual and West's (1999b) intellectual as artist/critic to explain creativity as the construct of the cultural repertoire of marginalized groups. In other words, it seems reasonable to talk about creativity in terms of cultural work considering (a) the repertoire construction of free spaces and (b) empowerment from cultural legacy.

The Creativity of Cultural Work

The creativity inherent in cultural work unfolds through specific notions that address the concerns central to the concept (e.g., the cultural repertoire, free spaces, and empowerment). Foucault's "specific" intellectual and West's intellectual as artist enlighten the understanding of the creativity of cultural work. Foucault (1984b) portrays the "specific" intellectual as one who interacts in the community to obtain immediate and concrete awareness of everyday problems specific to the challenges and struggles relevant to everyday people. These everyday people are in specific sectors of mainstream, middle- and low-income, and marginalized groups. The specific sectors Foucault references include yet are not limited to the family, the hospital, the university, and the church. He investigates the connection between theory and practice regarding "regimes of truth" (1984b, 73) (i.e., the complex relationship surrounding the types of discourse a society allows to function as true constituted over time and space). He describes this specific intellectual in the political sense as one who uses knowledge, competence, and relation to truth in the field of political struggles (1984b, 70) for everyday people in the specific sectors outlined. Since cultural traditions have institutional and cultural context developed over time and space (West 1999b) they are pivotal to the connection between theory, practice, and truth. West (1999b) interprets Foucault's specific intellectual as a new perspective, but also suggests a new portrayal of the intellectual as artist and critic (119–121). West elaborates by identifying his conception of the intellectual as artist and critic to be the cultural worker; one who is open to others (including the mainstream) yet focused and grounded in affirming and enabling subcultures of criticism. I believe Donald Schön (1983) enhances both Foucault's and West's conceptions as related to the creativity of cultural work through his articulation of reflective practice and practitioners.

Reflective Practice

The reflective practitioner makes sense of situations perceived as unique through discerning something already in existence in their repertoire (Schön 1983, 138). For example, the hooks/West (1991a, 1991b, 1991c) dialogue is an artful way in which two thinkers construct a repertoire that frames collective issues and bring critical rigor and context to the occasion through a group's cultural legacy. Walk into Your Season uses a cultural legacy in identifying similarities between the problem of slavery and youth transitioning from foster care. In both instances Schön permits us to understand the professional creativity endemic to cultural work. When confronted by inconsistent or incompatible demands (e.g., individualism vs. intergenerational sharing or communal unity vs. sexist division), a cultural worker responds by reflective practice about the appreciations they and others bring to the situation (Schön 1983, 62).

Creativity and Donald Schön's notion of reflective practice contribute to cultural work. Reflective practice starts with engaging in "a reflective conversation" (Schön 1983, 130). Faced with some issue, situation, or phenomenon, the reflective practitioner begins an inquiry on the problem. The phenomenon might resemble the concerns such as those bell hooks discloses in the hooks/West (1991b) dialogue. It might be making something (a smaller micro chip for example) or the inquiry might be framed as a problem to be understood (as in a research question guiding a study). The differences between these matters may be vast. That is, the inquiries can draw from diverse professional disciplines (Schön, 128). However the commonality is that the practitioner gives an artistic performance. The situation "comes to be understood through the attempt to change it, and changed through the attempt to understand it" (132). This means that the situation is changed by the action taken. In the case of hooks and West the previous lack of critical dialogue is mitigated by executing through Breaking Bread an exemplar of combined creativity and critical discourse in reflective practice. The situation is better understood as the cultural workers utilize the opportunity to change it. It is changed as they add to the body of work to attempt to understand it. Hooks and West change or at least reverse to some degree, the lack of discussion on troubling issues by initiating a dialogue about them. The critical dialogue evolves as artistry by enlisting creativity and traditional cultural expressions. Hooks and West gain understanding through the synergy of the dialogue and the dialogue stimulates audience reflection.

In Walk into Your Season the problem of moving from slavery and racial subordination is identified as a unique problem which has a parallel to transitioning from foster care. Where they differ is the role of free spaces. Cultural work differs in each setting because the black church has free spaces that may be renewed but foster care transition program has not yet developed them. Cultural work in both involved making something (audiovisuals, poetics). Constructing these creative pieces came through what Schön portrays as reflective practice about the appreciations cultural workers and others bring to the situation.

Through Foucault's (1984b) articulation of the "specific" intellectual as one committed to seeking truth about the social discourses that are accepted as accurate and legitimate where his or her conditions of work or life situate them; West's (1999b) portrayal of the intellectual as artist and critic; and Schön's (1983) reflective practitioner, the characteristics and modus operandi of the cultural worker as creative artist emerge and the related creative features of cultural work come into view. Creativity in cultural work is demonstrated through (1) the cultural worker's construction of a cultural repertoire that facilitates the conveyance and connection of the history, literature, and language of a culture, setting or movement ; (2) the cultural worker's potential to renew and create free spaces that facilitate individual and collective understanding through a cultural repertoire utilizing creative genres that may make use of empathy, shock, and action; and (3)the cultural worker's use of connection, form, appropriation, and collective memory in the creative genres utilized to facilitate individual and collective empowerment and action. Cultural legacy is central and utilized through the construction of a repertoire that is unveiled in free space.

Repertoire Construction of Free Spaces

A simple process first proposed by Graham Wallas (1926) in the *Art of Thought* has gained wide acceptance. According to Wallas, creative insights and illuminations may be explained by a process consisting of stages. These stages are fundamental to cultural work. They include (a) *preparation* (preparatory work on a problem that focuses the cultural worker's mind on the problem and explores the problem's dimensions), (b) *incubation* (where the problem is internalized into the cultural worker's unconscious mind and nothing appears externally to be happening), (c) *intimation* (the cultural worker gets a "feeling" that a solution is on its way), (d) insight or *illumination* (where the creative idea bursts forth from its preconscious processing into conscious awareness), and (e) *verification* (where the idea is consciously verified, elaborated, and then applied). Walk into Your Season exemplifies this process with parts b, c, and d operating simultaneously.

The creative process in cultural work involves preparatory work on a problem that focuses the cultural worker's mind on the dilemma and explores the problem's dimensions). In Walk into Your Season this was the critical and perhaps most important phase. I believe preparation in cultural work is ongoing. A cultural worker strives to perpetually observe, question, and expand understanding of cultural traditions so that knowledge about cultural history is internalized, enhanced, and readily available as part of an ongoing expansive repertoire. This need not be segregated to his or her own indigenous group, as in the case for me regarding youth transitioning from foster care. That withstanding, Walk into Your Season preparation began with my tacit awareness that I was doing something right in programs and workshops I was invited to facilitate. This tacit awareness was followed by my conscious attempt to scrutinize what I was doing and attempt to replicate it. The programs that I facilitated were well received. Attendee surveys attested to that. Through reflection I began to realize that in each successful program whether church, professional, or civic, (a) I spent a massive amount of time trying to understand the culture and community I was to address or work with, and (b) in most I created audiovisual accompaniments and inserted the symbols, people, poetics, music, and the traditions of the culture along with the intellectual content. Most of this was a tacit knowing of putting things together. There was no formal decision to do so and there was no formula. The time came however when I wanted to understand not only what was working but what was making it work. I began to simply think about the communities I was a part of, my earliest and ongoing recollections of those communities, the people instrumental in my involvement with those communities, and the music and images that moved me in those communities. I also watched other people responding to music and poetry and lyrics and community issues. And I began to look at old pictures and images of diverse groups. At this point, all the preparation was informal. My notes were loose and informal, yet not haphazard. However, it was the first time I can recall that as I read, thought, and looked at images, I wondered how a space is created. Further, what makes it empowering? This was simply the first inkling that maybe an idea was emerging through the preparation in the form of a question. Initially the question was simply how do these two communities (church and work) and my work in them relate to and edify one another? The question evolved, matured, and took root over time.

The creative process in cultural work also includes *incubation* (where the problem is internalized into the unconscious mind and nothing appears externally to be happening), *intimation* (when the cultural worker gets a "feeling" that a solution is on its way), and insight or *illumination* (where the creative idea bursts forth from its preconscious processing into the cultural worker's conscious awareness). These were not exactly separate phases for me. That is not to say this will always be the case or that others will experience the creative process the same way. For me it simply seemed that nothing was clicking (*incubation*) and then everything was clicking all at once (intimation and *illumination*). Spark plugs were firing, visions of what the two programs would look like flashed rapidly, and items and people to include came to mind. I began to write these things down and organize ideas more strategically and formally. From these notes the programs scripts, audiovisual scripts, and so forth evolved. I went from feeling that nothing was happening to feeling that everything was happening all at once.

The creative process in cultural work involves a time when the idea is consciously verified, elaborated, and then applied. The idea of Walk into Your Season was *consciously verified* when I researched and studied the concept of the cultural worker and approached the communities (Thirty-First Street and Richmond Social Services); *elaborated* as I constructed a creative cultural repertoire intrinsic to each setting considering the four related factors (cultural work, free space, discursive communities, and empowerment) and the creativity embedded in those factors; and then *applied* in scheduling dates and then executing the two programs in each setting. Initially I did not call it a repertoire. In fact, I did not know all of the terminology; however, I believed a creative concept was emerging. I now refer to the emergent creative product as "The Culturally Specific Creative Repertoire" which is an artistic collage of communal ingredients predicated on cultural legacy, free space, discursive communities, and empowerment and achieved through cultural work.

Empowerment from Cultural Legacy

Synthesizing the commonality in empowerment theories, the creativity of cultural work, and the nature of the discursive community reveals that cultural work which facilitates empowerment from cultural legacy (a) is a creative process that involves preparation; (b) is communal; (c) involves active participation, critical reflection, and awareness; and (d) involves access to and control over important decisions and resources. Building on the notion of creativity, *Walk into Your Season* conceives that the creativity of cultural work endeavors the renewal and creation of free space and fosters empowerment in a discursive community. The cultural work of the hooks/West dialogue is insightful.

Cultural Work and the "hooks/West" Method

The creativity of cultural work is illustrated in the efforts of bell hooks and Cornel West. Hooks and West use cultural elements of a tradition to stimulate discussion in a project which eventually evolved into the book *Breaking Bread*. The dialogue transcript reflects the inclusion of music and its relationship to community, testimony, and critical conversation (hooks and West 1991b). The dialogue fuses creativity and lived experience. Hooks embarks upon a public conversation with colleague Cornell West stating that in part:

Cornel and I conceived of the initial dialogue we did together in public as a way to intervene on the kind of sexist divisions that have been historically constructed between Black men and Black women. To present ourselves as living examples of the will on the part of both Black men and women to talk with one another, to process, and engage in rigorous intellectual and political dialogue (hooks and West 1991b, 3). We engage in a playful interrogation that is part of the *joie de vivre* we want to bring to our sense of what it means to be Black intellectuals at this historical moment. (4)

West adds that this kind of action can empower other people who take the life of the mind seriously and link it to spiritual and political struggle (hooks and West 1991b, 4). West also references the historical perception of the intellectual. Historically discerned and described to varying degrees as haughty, arrogant, and elitist, the hooks/West dialogue offers an opportunity to reflect, break down, and reframe the historical image of the intellectual, exposing some of the faults and foibles as well as the insights, contributions, and appreciations that hooks and West bring to the table (4).

It is significant that the repertoire of the hooks/West dialogue unfolds in the community. [H]ooks explains that the spirit of testimony is a difficult spirit to convey in writing (hooks and West 1991b, 1). However after her first dialogue with West at Yale it struck her that dialogue is a way in which the sense of mutual witness and testimony can manifest (1) [H]ooks says the "Learning to Question" dialogues of Paulo Freire and Antonio Faundez (1989) theoretically introduced her to the notion of collectivity and moved her to consider what it means to talk with one another and engage some type of collaborative response (hooks and West 1991b, 3).

[H]ooks and West construct a repertoire from the African American cultural legacy. They bring this repertoire and the Breaking Bread dialogue into communal intimacy. Believing that reclaiming history is a prerequisite for sharing and creating community bonds in the twenty-first century, their goal was to create a community at the Yale gathering that would be a place to promote understanding (hooks and West 1991b, 8). Before this audience they expose, discuss, and grapple with community issues, naming the experience Breaking Bread.

As a result, the hooks/West dialogue benefits from self-imposed reflection and progresses through connections manifested through cultural expressions. [H]ooks and West use a repertoire of traditionally familiar language, music, and creativity to approach the discussion. In the vein of jazz musicians, they manifest a "feel for" their material and make on the spot adjustments. Their collective effort resembles the musical invention that makes good use of schema familiar to all participants. In addition, just as each jazz musician has a ready repertoire that can be delivered at appropriate moments (Schön 1983), so too do hooks and West. In other words, hooks and West through joint reflection also find context in expressions that bring painful issues of race, gender, and power dynamics to the forefront in a nonincendiary manner. The historical context is inserted as is their lived experience and the contemporary nexus is articulated through their research, observations, and cultural expressions.

An example of this contextualized reflection using culturally derived repertoire comes prior to the beginning of the program proper when hooks summons someone to sing "Precious Lord." The song was written by Thomas A. Dorsey, whose legacy is his instrumental role in shaping gospel music. (Parenthetically, gospel was at one time scorned due to its jazz inflection.) The conditions prompting Dorsey to pen the song are legendary and saturated in heart wrenching pain; the catalyst is the death of his wife in childbirth. Initially Dorsey finds consolation in the news that the baby survives. Shortly thereafter he learns that the infant has succumbed also. Like anyone looking forward to the dual happiness of marriage and parenthood, Dorsey hoped for a different outcome and a very different future. However, rather than immediate deliverance from the circumstance, Dorsey receives something that speaks beyond his personal situation, transcends the moment, and has comforted generation to generation, culture to culture, and gender to gender. Somehow in the midst of his emotional turmoil Dorsey pours out a counter narrative through the song "Precious Lord Take My Hand." It encourages people feeling trapped and defeated in the dips, valleys and vicissitudes of life. It has since been passed from movement to movement and community to community. It was the song often requested by Dr. Martin Luther King, including prior to a scheduled meeting that would never convene due to the leader's assassination. It was the song sung at bell hooks' grandmother's funeral. It was and is a song that conjures memories of gender, the fragility of life, and faith in the midst of crisis. It is a song invested in "the knowledge that we can take our pain, work with it, recycle it, and transform it so that it becomes a source of power" (hooks and West 1991b, 8). [H]ooks is able to make a collective parallel through an individual entity that has widespread common understanding.

[H]ooks's ability to jumpstart a dialogue using a traditional song transcends culture (the song is familiar beyond the African American community), yet exemplifies the creativity of cultural work. Her insight crafts a demonstration of the utilization of a song in creative artistry. Another example of this creativity occurs early in the introduction when hooks recalls the spirit of testimony embedded in a traditional song often linked to the communion ritual in the black church. "Let Us Break Bread Together on Our Knees ... When I Fall on My Knees with My Face to the Rising Sun, Oh Lord Have Mercy on Me." She conveys the synergy of an unquestionably personal thus primarily individual story (*When I Fall*), accessible to others through the notion of a community of faith (*Let Us Break Bread Together*) yet relating the mercy (*Have Mercy on Me*) that summons the "compassion, acceptance, understanding, and empathy" (hooks and West 1991b, 1–2) accessible to the individual and the collective.

West responds by recalling a rhythm and blues song by Fred Wesley and the JBs entitled "Breaking Bread," which according to West, deals with critical recovery and critical revision of one's past, traditions, history, and heritage (hooks and West, 2). After the song and an explanation regarding context, hooks tells her fellow cultural worker Cornell West that together they bring to the occasion a willingness to engage intellectually with a critical affirmation that allows them to talk, argue, disagree, "even become disappointed in one another, yet still leave one another with a sense of joy and spiritual renewal" (2). They articulate the goal of this conversation as a shared discussion with a community of faith. This does not mean the creation of a religious community but rather a community of comrades seeking to deepen their understanding of life, political experience, and spiritual experience (hooks and West 1991b). In evoking that sense of breaking bread, these cultural workers enlist the various traditions of sharing that take place in domestic, secular, and sacred life where people come together to give of ourselves to one another fully, to nurture life, to renew their spirits, sustain their hope, and make a lived politics of revolutionary struggle an ongoing practice (hooks and West 1991b, 6).

Implicit in this sense of breaking bread is the construction of a repertoire using cultural traditions. The worker draws on his or her repertoire—the artistic, intuitive processes that practitioners bring to situations of problem solving (Schön 1983, 49). The dialogue between hooks and West is an example of the work of two cultural workers artistically, critically and intentionally grappling with complex topics and hard questions. It personifies intellectuals fluent in the cultural expressions of tradition yet very much engaged in the life of the mind, writing, reading, and so on. Hooks and West as cultural workers bring cultural traditions and lived experience to their dialogue in order to engage and break bread. The range and variety of their creative repertoire (songs, music, language, traditions, etc.) enables these workers to utilize their past experience and the traditions of their lived experience in order to explore and have a feel for problems that do not fit the existing rules.

I have considered creativity as the construct of the cultural repertoire of marginalized groups. The interplay between culture and creativity creates the conditions through which cultural work, free spaces, discursive communities, and empowerment evolve. The role of a cultural worker is to remain conscious of this interplay and mine resources. This includes building cultural repertoires that renew and initiate the role of free spaces in discursive communities in order to achieve empowerment from cultural legacy.

Chapter 3: Cultural Work and the Methods of Walk into Your Season

Imagination is the chief instrument of the good ... art is more moral than moralities. For the latter either are, or tend to become, consecrations of the status quo, reflections of custom, reinforcements of the established order. The moral prophets of humanity have always been poets even though they spoke in free verse or by parable ... Art has been the means of keeping alive the sense of purposes that outrun evidence and of meanings that transcend indurated habit.

—John Dewey, *Art As Experience*

[W]e have an opportunity [to move] beyond the Old World concept of race, class, and caste, to create, finally, what we must have had in mind when we first began speaking of the New World. But the price of this is a long look backward [from] when we came and an unflinching assessment of the record. For an artist, the record of that journey is most clearly revealed in the personalities [and work] of the people the journey produced.

—James Baldwin, *The Creative Process*

This chapter is divided into four parts. Part one describes the repertoire building of cultural work as creativity informed by the "hooks/West" method; the kinds of discussion that occurs in free spaces; and building the repertoire of the discursive community so that people feel empowered. Part two expresses the personal dimensions of cultural work through tacit knowledge (a concept meaning that we bring more that we can express to a situation) and reflective practice. Part three puts theory into practice through explaining the salient decisions of Walk into Your Season. Part four explains reflective practice as the method of identifying the effective practice of cultural work.

Drawing from the "hooks/West" Method

Scholarly practitioners bell hooks and Cornel West use cultural legacy to construct a repertoire. This repertoire emerges through historical traditions and the interplay of creativity, culture, historical context, personal experience, rigor, power, and empowerment. [H]ooks and West conduct a dialogue in order to explore a framework where people theorize experience in such a way so as to understand trauma beyond the sole emotional experience of the tragedy (hooks and West 1991c, 34). They articulate theirs as a perspective that responds to historical and contemporary pain in an improvisational, creative manner that allows people to survive and thrive (34). Both hooks and West inform our understanding of collective trauma that bears individual impact and the need to preserve the historical relevance of lessons learned yet discern contemporary significance and empowering practices.

For instance hooks and West reflect upon specific symbols and repertoires indigenous to the black church as an institution in their Breaking Bread dialogue and acknowledge the effect of historical and traditional cultural influences in shaping, empowering, and inspiring their personal and professional trajectories. Their repertoire includes traditions such as testimony, preaching and the musical roots of gospel and jazz music. Testimony, for example, is an integral part of the black religious tradition. It is personal yet accessible to the community. It not only strengthens the individual but also builds a faith of the community. A personal dimension of testimony and a collective biographical account come together in the repertoire.

Similarly, the personal dimension of testimony, collective biography, and empowering leadership converged as I developed the creative repertoire of Walk into Your Season. There were traditional cultural influences (historical legacy, musical genres, artistry, leadership, church) that played a central role in shaping, empowering, and inspiring my personal and professional aspirations. My recollections often went to the late Dr. Darrel Rollins. Dr. Rollins was the pastor of Thirty-First Street for over twenty-five years. He encouraged me to explore and develop my talents, both academic and professional. He entrusted certain tasks that empowered me to use my speaking abilities and writing skills. In reflection, I realize that he was encouraging me to grow and align my skills with my tacit awareness of the community. Dr. Rollins introduced me to Dr. Wyatt Tee Walker, a venerable leader who was chief of staff to Dr. Martin Luther King and who often spoke at Thirty-First Street. When I initially conceived Walk into Your Season, I went to Dr. Walker's home to discuss my nascent idea. At the time I had forgotten that he is also an ethnomusicologist. He listened carefully and inspired me to pursue my idea due to the potential in exploring cultural legacy. At that meeting he and Mrs. Walker talked about their experiences in the black church as an institution. They described the church as a space that empowered them during the dark days of the civil rights movement. Both Dr. and Mrs. Walker spoke with a dignified calm and peacefulness as if they savored a sweet triumph. Knowing what they had endured I wondered how they could do so. Initially I may have even thought it absurd. However their attitude made sense when I reflected on my childhood, my parents, and Rev. Warren A. Page of Emanuel A.M.E. Church in Portsmouth, Virginia. In Emanuel the song "Peace Be Still" emerged as a favorite in a church that was a safe space built by slaves. I conceived Dr. Rollins and Dr. Walker and Rev. Page as cornerstones in a cultural legacy. Walk into Your Season is not based solely on them but perhaps would not have come to fruition without them. Due to their (Drs. Rollins and Walker) direct influence on my work I decided to include them in the audiovisual component of the Walk into Your Season Thirty-First Street program.

While hooks and West express and focus upon a potentially helpful repertoire of tools and traditions, some of these traditions have been portrayed as oral and improvisational. Their potential as creative genres building repertoires of renewing empowering properties useful in problem solving to address barriers, issues, and challenges in discursive communities is often underestimated. As such they go unnoticed, unexplored, unmentioned, or simply omitted (Gaventa and Pettit 2010; Evans 2010; West 1991). However, the traditions have institutional and cultural context developed over time and space (West 1991).

The artistry of selecting cultural items and building a repertoire of empowerment around them is the central reason I drew from the hooks/West Breaking Bread dialogue in conceptualizing Walk into Your Season. For example, their use of traditional songs from a cultural legacy influenced what I conceived to be appropriate in Walk into Your Season. Consider the song "Lift Every Voice and Sing," which is central to the repertoire of the Thirty-First Street Church event. Writer James Weldon Johnson tells a story of recovery and revision, reflects and recaptures the pride in that story, and renews a sense of hope and empowerment in the discursive community. The song tells a collective story of overcoming adversity, inspiring the audience to lift their voices as a community, affirming and claiming the pride of survival. ("God of our weary years, God of our silent tears, Thou who has brought us thus far on our way ... Shadowed beneath Thy hand may we forever stand, True to our God true to our native land.") Similarly, focusing on youth transitioning from foster care into adulthood, the counterpart in the Walk into Your Season social work program contextualized the diverse individual conceptions of empowerment within an overarching collective theme. The song "Amazing Grace" spoke to individual hope and transformation within a communal context for understanding a collective sentiment. ("Through many dangers toils and snares I have already come; 'Tis grace hath brought me safe thus far and grace will lead me home.") I used it in the social work program because it a song reminiscent of John Newton's dark past yet jubilant about a grace that transcends the darkness of slavery and adverse circumstances. Likewise, in the foster care program, the song "Bridge over Troubled Waters" spoke to the individual and collective empowerment available in transition alongside solace and help in the midst of oppression. ("All your dreams are on their way; See how they shine; If you need a friend I'm sailing right behind. Like a bridge over troubled water, I will ease your mind.")

As I contemplated the cultural legacy I conceived the poetic repertoire. In the audiovisual I decided to use Langston Hughes's "The Negro Speaks of Rivers" (which conveys the soul deep intricacies of a collective history); Paul Laurence Dunbar's "We Wear the Mask" (which reveals the pain of disguise); and Countee Cullen's "Incident" (which articulates the deep memory of childhood hurt); and I paraphrased Margaret Walker's "For My People" (which is an inspirational historical recollection of the power of hope). Walt Whitman's "I Hear America Singing" illustrates the beauty of the democratic landscape in the audiovisual, while Langston Hughes's "I Too Sing America" offers a another vantage point (from the kitchen) yet a vantage point which facilitates the opportunity to grow stronger and become empowered. William Herbert Carruth's poem "Each in His Own Tongue" expresses the integration of varied experiences and interpretations embodied in personal lived experience within the collective journey. I wrote the poem "There's a Transformation," which invites the listener to reinvent themselves and step into a new role.

Examining the Hooks-West dialogue in the book *Breaking Bread*, and the fundamental notion of Breaking Bread that unfolds, I saw some specifics that I believed should be integral to the Walk into Your Season concept.

1. *The* Breaking Bread *dialogue shows scholars reflecting on their personal narratives before an audience, and openly revealing how their own lives factor into their work (as well as in some instances how it is appropriately and justifiably inseparable from their work).* In Walk into Your Season, I identify the problem of moving from slavery and racial subordination and propose that the problem has a parallel to transitioning from foster care. This gives rise to Walk into Your Season—the journey. Reflecting on this parallel from my standpoint as a woman of African American descent with personal history in the black church as well as a practitioner in foster care, I began to consider the notion of contextualizing renewal in one community (Thirty-First Street Baptist Church) and creating the role of free space in another (youth transitioning from foster care in Richmond Social Services). Renewal and creativity present an opportunity to move beyond conceptual restraints regarding caste, class, and race by reflecting on the record and the people of the journey.

2. *The* Breaking Bread *dialogue reveals scholars acknowledging a relationship to the discursive community and the desire to see people thrive (which I conceive as the desire to locate and implement empowering practices).* As the Walk into Your Season cultural worker my relationship with the respective discursive communities came through my membership in the Thirty-First Street Baptist Church and as an education practitioner in foster care. The foster care history in the social service setting had a different breadth and texture. Certainly, poems and music with a history conducive to conveying an inspiring message were appropriate. However, the trajectory of the social work history is far younger than that of the Thirty-First Street discursive community, whose history is entwined with that of the black church as an institution. The

historical context of the social work setting relates to the story and plight of Willie Palmer and his courage in becoming empowered to take a stand for youth aging out of foster care. Therefore the sequence of program elements pursuant to the social work setting attempts to at once illuminate (the history) and enlighten (the audience) with regard to establishing and distilling a counter narrative to the pain of Willie Palmer. The counter narrative highlights what Palmer was able to achieve in spite of his circumstance. The hope was that a community pulse and resonating theme would evolve. As the cultural worker I revealed the historical journey through a repertoire of records, personalities, artists, and artistic contributions. My tacit knowledge was helpful in recognizing lost and hidden knowledge and the awareness of internalized oppression.

3. *The* Breaking Bread *dialogue demonstrates scholars revealing the willingness to discuss cultural matters, sometimes employing traditional tools like indigenous music in nontraditional ways (like using a song to open the dialogue).* In the case of the Walk into Your Season Thirty-First Street setting I did not conceive that historical entities or genres had been totally forgotten. Rather, I conceived them as becoming matter of fact, suggesting a case for renewal. Intrinsic value was overlooked or no longer esteemed because the value was either lurking behind untold stories or subsumed by painful memories for which counter narratives were not inserted. Wisdom transmission was thin. Looking back and considering that the spirituals for instance were the first artistic gift of Afro-Americans to the world, and the fact that they illustrate existential freedom in action (West 1999a) meant that the use of music in creating the space was paramount. For example, many people were unaware of the historical trajectory and legacy of "Lift Every Voice and Sing." It was an institutional anchor and a community vehicle for individual

and collective empowerment. The lyrics penned by James Weldon Johnson began as a poem in 1899 and was originally written by Johnson for a presentation in celebration of the birthday of Abraham Lincoln. The lyrics were set to music by James Weldon Johnson's brother John. Since the song was originally performed in Jacksonville, Florida, by children it seemed fitting that a child would lead it in the Walk into Your Season program.

4. *The* Breaking Bread *dialogue reveals intentional willingness and conscious planning in order to initiate a dialogue for discussing their reflections and contextualizing the traditions, symbols, and rituals of the discursive community with contemporary issues.* I created an audiovisual collage of images, poetry, music, and narration for each event. Choirs performed. Spiritual, jazz, and blues inflections could be heard in their renditions. This is relevant as gospel is a derivative of the spirituals and jazz. Two choirs (Thirty-First Street and Virginia Commonwealth University's Black Awakening Choir) brought different interpretations of the musical genre to the occasion. While the venerable, more traditional Thirty-First Street choir was chosen because of their traditional repertoire, the Black Awakening Choir ushered a new generation into the occasion, aligned with the theme of renewing the historical role of free space. The choirs' inspirational music countered the images in the audiovisual that may have been troubling for some people.

5. *The* Breaking Bread *dialogue brings the conversation to the community and presents issues with candor and the spontaneity of unscripted conversation.* I created and organized Walk into Your Season as two community events. There were parts of Walk into Your Season that were unscripted yet the spontaneity highlighted community issues. The spontaneity of unscripted conversation was

evident in the reception. Participant's described it as a space in which community conversation could take place. In the church program an intergenerational theme unfolded in an unscripted part of the program. One of the founders of the Black Awakening Choir attended the event. As I recollect the occasion, I feel that her presence symbolized contributions made to the renewal of the historical role of free space since people continue the tradition. I asked her to stand so the audience could receive her and acknowledge her contribution. Due to her vision along with others, the choir remains perpetually replenished by a cadre of new students.

6. *The* Breaking Bread *dialogue scholars take the risk of disclosing their own personal and professional vulnerabilities as related to cultural work.* As stated, in Walk into Your Season I created an audiovisual collage of images, poetry, music, and narration for each event. In the church audiovisual, lines from Walt Whitman and Langston Hughes poems ("I Hear America Singing" and "I Too Sing America," respectively) are inserted into the collage and capture the different lenses through which two artists see and illustrate America. Likewise people see the journey of youth transitioning from foster care through different lenses and some people ignore the journey of those youth altogether. The historical poetic exchange between Whitman and Hughes simultaneously expresses the creativity of cultural work, the creative value of the artists' perspectives, and the relevance of culturally diverse perceptions. However, it also expresses the vulnerability of invisibility and begs the question, what does a person do with the emotion of rejection when overlooked or marginalized, whether intended or unintentional? Can he or she find healing and solutions in the discursive community? Finally, in terms of vulnerability,

does the cultural worker take a risk in both communities by exposing gaps in the real and the perceived?

7. *The* Breaking Bread *dialogue scholars do not proselytize religion but they do talk about the church as an institution.* The Walk into Your Season journey looks back at the black church and the notion of double consciousness that W. E. B. Du Bois spells out in his seminal work. This reflection led me to understand how the church as an institution became an antibody for black invisibility, namelessness, and vulnerability. Rather than relegation to abstraction, objects of scorn, and perennial substatus as a problem people inhabiting a world divided by a thick wall ("Veil") requiring mask wearing and role playing (as opposed to genuine human interaction), the black church was a space acknowledging black people for what they were: a people with problems rather than a problem people. Reflecting upon the church as an institution in terms of its historical role as a free space, the notion of creating the Walk into Your Season events began to coalesce. I portray the black church as an institution characterized by intrinsic properties inherent in its historical role and revitalized in the hooks/West dialogue.

The Kinds of Discussions that Occur in Free Space

Scholars hooks and West use traditional cultural expressions to set the stage for critical engagement in dialogues that seek to empower a community. They begin with problem identification. [H]ooks, for example, recalls the disbelief an acquaintance expresses when hooks shares the desire to purchase a home beside her parent's home. Hooks interprets this individual's disbelief as an inability to grasp or appreciate the value of sharing intergenerational family life, a mindset that according to hooks signals a looming crisis. In another instance hooks considers historically constructed sexist divisions between African American men and women (hooks and West 1991b). She perceives a community and institutional crisis that plays a fundamental role in transmitting cultural values and sensibility, ways of life, and ways of struggle, and as a consequence people are distanced from predecessors and from critical tasks at hand (hooks and West 1991b, 10). After identifying this problem she ponders the lack of critical discussion about the problem, that is, the lack of discussion about the communal tensions and social conditions she observes in her community and those discerned problematic in her scholarly work. She fears that African Americans no longer recognize as valuable the notion of collectively shaping the terms of survival and empowerment, and she portrays this as a crisis (hooks and West 1991b).

Building the Repertoire of the Discursive Community So People Feel Empowered

Building a repertoire that empowers people facilitates empowered settings.

The work of Maton and Salem (1995) discussed in Chapter 2 informs my understanding of these settings.

1. *An empowering setting demonstrates leadership that is inspirational, visionary, shared, and committed to the community.* As the cultural worker in Walk into Your Season, I attempted to construct an empowering setting using methods of creativity and repertoire building to facilitate renewal of a free space in one discursive community and to create a free space in another. To contextualize the shared history of the discursive community I use a creative repertoire that includes community members to provide a frame of reference. For instance, the "church" lady regaled in her hat enters the sanctuary on a syncopated beat and

demonstrates a proud walk. She is at once a symbol of cultural pride and leadership. Writing her role into the script as leading the choir to their destination was conceived to energize and inspire. A collective story from individual experiences emerges as well as a counter narrative. In the IL program, the involvement and presence of the social workers conveyed the interest, commitment, and shared leadership. The foster care supervisor spoke, brought his wife, and also brought a youth with him.

2. *An empowering setting cultivates resources that activate personal resources and participation.* I attempted to construct an empowering setting in the Walk into Your Season church setting by asking for the church families' involvement and participation. I submitted a letter to the pastor requesting a meeting. After I obtained his approval and an endorsement of the research I had to meet with the joint board (deaconate and trustees). I gave a presentation that revisited the role of the church as an institution, portraying it as a free space. I explained the role of free spaces in the community. I also talked about empowerment in the presentation, explaining that my research asks whether the historical role of the space could be renewed or created in other settings. I attempted to construct an empowering setting in the Walk into Your Season social work setting, beginning by contacting the independent living foster care supervisor at the Richmond Department of Social Services (RDSS), asking if it was alright to approach the appropriate social workers regarding Walk into Your Season. I then set up a meeting to present my project and to ask for support and participation. After obtaining his support and approval I then approached social workers at the Richmond Department of Social Services, did a presentation to explain the program concept, sent correspondence, made myself

available to answer questions, and always explained that I needed the social workers' help, involvement, and feedback. The social work supervisor participated in the program. He addressed the audience and told his story regarding the connection between his background and his reason for being involved with the youth transitioning from foster care. I attempted to construct empowering settings for both events through the writing of program scripts focused on the two discursive communities. I also conceived and created audiovisual products to bring a visual dimension to the poetry, stories, and historical episodes. I invited the Virginia Commonwealth University gospel choir, Thirty-First Street Baptist Church Choir, church leaders, civic and social workers, youth, and administrators. I believed participation and attendance by these groups exemplified the cultivation desired in an empowering setting. Each however symbolized a community/cultural connection in some way. Most important as related to the social work program was inviting the youth to tell their stories. The youth publicly expressed their gratitude to the community for listening to their stories, which was perhaps more powerful than anything else I could have done to cultivate resources and illustrate community participation in an empowering setting.

3. *An empowering setting is one that fosters critical awareness, transcends self-concern, includes individual, organizational, and community narratives, and focuses on member strengths should be evident.* I attempted to construct an empowering setting in Walk into Your Season by articulating a critical awareness and revealing a belief system through four related factors: (a) cultural work, (b) free space, (c), discursive communities, and (d) empowerment. Relying on cultural legacy, I scripted narratives revealing individual, communal, and organizational stories that emerged through cultural

work in the two setting. I chose the images, music, and songs I included in the scripted narrative and program through a creative process because I found them to at once speak a collective yet individual yet intergenerational language. For instance, in the IL setting a song like "Bridge Over Troubled Waters" is a reminder of personal survival and the power of communal support. I also chose people to demonstrate their strengths. For example, the social workers selected two youth participants and I selected one. I called each one prior to the program and discussed the program and their role in it. I made sure they could ask any questions they had and that they had my number and email address should they want to do so.

4. *An empowering setting provides a supportive group climate marked by shared events, celebrations, and ritual.* I attempted to construct an empowering setting by creating the two Walk into Your Season events which were celebrations of renewal, creativity, and community. I have observed celebrations and rituals in the church community for as long as I can remember. Historically, recitals, teas, Holy Communion, revival, Children's Day, church anniversary have been familiar rituals and celebrations in the life of the church. These were times and spaces for community affirmation and reflection. People could share their time and their talents. In fact, the words appearing on the Walk into Your Season printed program read "celebrating free spaces." As times change it seems relevant to change with the times, yet never lose the strength embedded in history. For example, when the Thirty-First Street Baptist Church burned down in the 1960s, the church community came together to rebuild. The first church was obtained through a member mortgaging his home. When that church burned down the current edifice was built and the congregation celebrated by marching from the school where they had

temporarily worshiped into the new sanctuary. They turned an obstacle into an opportunity. The only thing salvageable from the old church was the bell. The ritual of breaking ground and then cutting the ribbon at the doors, and the celebration of walking to the new sanctuary empowered the community. They carried the old bell to the new church. It sits on the grounds today. An official told me that the bell symbolized all that they still had and what they had accomplished together. Rather than casting traditions aside the collective memory of cultural legacy is maintained through renewal and aids the creation of new legacies in emergent communities. I attempted to recall and reconsider old stories and create new ones. Fortunately I did not have to rely on my memory and observations alone. There were pictures, old printed programs, church history that I obtained from the church clerk, deacons, trustees, and older members. Experiences and aspirations were shared by younger members and youth transitioning from foster care. Event history in the case of social services was recalled by social workers who shared stories about successes as well as failures. With their help I attempted to remember (and re-member) in order to renew in the Thirty-First Street event and create a space in the social services event. The reception became a free space where people could express themselves and food was symbolic of the communal tradition of Breaking Bread.

Tacit Knowledge and Cultural Work

In addition to the intentional and deliberate elements of cultural work, it also has a tacit dimension. Like other forms of skillful action, cultural work may reveal that people often know more than they can express (Schön 1983, 51). Alfred Schultz (1961) portrays this as the everyday tacit know-how people bring to ordinary social interactions. Michael Polyani (1967) popularized the phrase "tacit knowing" to describe the prelogical phase of knowing, arguing that we should start from the fact that "we can know more than we can tell."

Central to Polanyi's thinking is the belief that creative acts (especially acts of discovery) are charged with strong personal feelings and commitments. He portrays the process of discovery as one which inevitably allows us to understand the way that many bits of tacit knowledge can be brought together to help form a new model or theory. By paying attention to Polanyi's conception of the tacit dimension we can begin to make sense of the place of intuition and hunches in informal practice and how we can come to a better understanding of what might be going on in different situations.[2]

I believe this to be the case with Walk into Your Season which at first glance illustrates autoethnography since the researcher is (a) a full member in the research group or setting, (b) visible as such a member, and (c) committed to developing theoretical understandings of broader social phenomena (Anderson 2006). Both autoethnography and tacit knowing recognize a personal connection with the subject under study. However, the cultural work of Walk into Your Season goes beyond exploring personal experience indicative of autoethnography (Reed-Danahay 1997). I investigate traditional ideas and their values. An example can be found in my decisions regarding the *Walk into Your Season* creative elements. In deciding on the program elements I would write myself and those program components that would be better served by using traditional pieces written by others I had a gut feeling regarding what I believed would work—a *hunch*.

Though this *hunch* was informed I had neither defined nor articulated it as part of a creative process. Polyani (1967) argues

---

2 Smith, M. K. (2003). "Michael Polanyi and Tacit Knowledge," *The Encyclopedia of Informal Education*. Retrieved from http://www.infed.org/thinkers/polanyi.htm.

that while imaginings, hunches, and informed guesses are part of exploratory acts aimed at discovering "truth," they are not necessarily in a form that can be articulated in propositional or formal terms. I made these decisions regarding traditional ideas and their values pertinent to the creativity of Walk into Your Season relying on my historical research on the discursive communities, people I knew, recalling my childhood experiences in Emanuel A.M.E. Church as well as Thirty-First Street, observing how people at diverse programs respond to music and verse in religious and nonreligious settings, and observing the foster care community, and a gut instinct of what worked and what did not. For instance I decided that I could not conceive of writing anything more adequately expressive and symbolic of African American collective history, pride, and empowerment than "Lift Every Voice." On the other hand I felt that my own writing and audiovisual creation could best complement the foundation that "Lift Every Voice" established. Likewise I felt that since the goal was creating a space in the social work program, writing the accompanying script for the audiovisual and creating a poem on transformation made good sense. These innovative tools were designer originals created to address an emerging community. Based on all of that, I never ruled out the power of an informed hunch. This suggests that tacit knowing demonstrates the spontaneity of judgment and recognition; recognition of lost or hidden knowledge; and the awareness of internalized understandings

The cultural work of *Walk into Your Season* examines shared constructions of experience as products of action, as conditioning elements for future action, and in structuring one's perception of the world or shaping behavior (as in the case of morals, customs, and laws). In other words, cultural work is predicated upon the tacit knowledge about a group's experience acquired through individual experience rather than a focus on an individual experience within a group.

Frame Analysis

Donald Schön (1983) says that frame analysis studies the ways practitioners frame roles and problems. The concept of frame analysis can be traced back to the sociology of knowledge, particularly the work of Karl Mannheim (1936). Mannheim's work considers how specific views of reality evolve out of specific groups. According to Schön, frame analysis can help practitioners in gaining awareness of their tacit frames and also in criticizing these tacit frames (309). If practitioners on the other hand remain unaware, they do not attend to the ways they construct the realities in which they function and the construct simply becomes a given (310). Schön informs the understanding of this concept in relationship to the cultural worker in that a cultural worker becomes aware of alternative ways of framing. Once the frames and roles are discerned, alternative frames and approaches can be developed to assist in establishing the cultural worker's role and potential efficacy in developing solutions. For example, to explore aspects of free space and discursive communities, Walk into Your Season looks at renewing the role of free spaces by a cultural worker to a new generation in a discursive community that empowers people as well as the initiation of free spaces in a new community. Mihalyi Csikszentmihalyi (1997) further enhances and informs my understanding of Schön's notion of reflective practice and the related creativity cultural workers bring to exploration. Csikszentmihalyi considers the kind of creativity that leaves a trace in the cultural matrix (23). He conceives creativity through the lens of place rather than merely product. Csikszentmihalyi informs this exploration through his perception that creativity is not "what is it, but where is it" (27). This overarching conceptualization frames and contextualizes the issue and positions the *Walk into Your Season* settings for analysis. Focus group members responded to questions subsumed under this overarching frame.

Theory to Practice: The Salient Decisions of *Walk into Your Season*

Walk into Your Season examines cultural work that can empower members of a community using methods of creativity and repertoire building taken from the work of bell hooks and Cornell West. Personal dimensions of knowledge acquired through tacit knowing and reflective practice are also used. The creativity of cultural work intends to foster discussion in the discursive community to enhance empowerment through a creative synergy of stories, histories, images, narratives, music, people, practices, and artistic mediums. I conceive this creative synergy as a repertoire. Constructing the repertoire involved a number of decisions.

The multitude of decisions related to Walk into Your Season span the gamut from minuscule to momentous. Careful consideration of the decisions and the impact of these decisions on the respective discursive communities reveals the dimensions of the repertoire. There are instances in constructing the repertoire where the knowledge is tacit and spontaneous, instances when lost or hidden knowledge is recognized, and instances when the awareness of internalized understandings surfaces.

Renewing on the history of free space in the black church of the African American community and trying to create a discursive community in another setting were distinct tasks. Two programs in separate venues were necessary. This is due to the need to distinguish, illustrate, and focus on the precise elements of the study in the two respective communities. Here I share a few of the decisions that bear the most significant impact.

How did I decide on the two group settings (i.e., discursive communities)?

I wanted to draw on the history of free space as a source of renewal in one discursive community in order to create the practice in a different setting. The black church as an institution exemplified what I discerned as a free space. As a practitioner I was familiar with the challenges youth transitioning from foster care confront. As such these two communities fit my research criteria in the city in which I lived and whose work and challenges I was familiar.

Why the black church and why one in which I am a member?

Due to its history as an institution, the black church seemed to me a fertile vessel through which to attempt Walk into Your Season. This decision was again based on the project focus: Can a cultural worker renew the role of free spaces to a new generation in a discursive community that empowers people or create it in a new community? My familiarity with the black church as an institution dates back to childhood recollections of Emanuel A.M.E. Church. As an adult I am a member of Thirty-First Street Baptist Church. Access to people, resources, and memories that might be helpful as I pursued the study was important.

What is the creative product? Why did I decide to create a program with multiple creative pieces (a creative collage in free space) rather than a single entity (like a poem)?

I decided to so because a community is a creative collage. I believe that a community is full of different elements, people, dynamics, and talents. The creative repertoire that emerges from this collage is in my view what facilitates, renews, and creates free spaces. The emergent creative product is "The Culturally Specific Creative Repertoire" (CSCR), which I consider to be a genre. It is an artistic collage of communal ingredients predicated on cultural legacy, free space, discursive communities and empowerment and achieved through cultural work.

Why two programs?

Two programs were necessary to illustrate and focus on the precise elements of the study in the two respective communities. Drawing on the history of free space in the black church of the African American community and trying to create a discursive community were separate tasks that called for two programs.

Where should the events be held?

I decided to use my own church site. I was familiar with the site, many of the congregants, and could efficiently address logistical matters as they arose. I also wanted them (the discursive community) to feel that they had ownership in the program, because they did, both as a product of history and as a history maker. The church had six people integral to the Walk into Your Season logistics (two for sound, one for security, one for the building, and two for administrative direction and assistance) all of whom I was very familiar. The Children's Museum was the other site chosen. I had worked with the staff before and recalled that their commitment to foster care and adoption came as the result of a staff person's direct experience. Their fees were reasonable, but most of all, the metaphor of having the program at a site dedicated to children felt like the right thing to do. One space is claimed/created and the other is invited.

Was I prepared and confident enough to support my case for significance in the event my committee and significant others (academic community, social work community) questioned the relevance of the concept?

Yes. I had to ask myself this question as the answer would impact my commitment to stay the course. I decided that as the rigor of deeper engagement with the concepts ensued and my conversations with scholars familiar with the concept progressed, my knowledge and confidence would increase. I believed and anticipated that the committee would direct me well and supply the guidance I needed and that their prompts and inquiries would enhance the work as it bolstered my confidence. Nevertheless, I only came to a decision after seeking wise counsel from the academic community (Dr. Norma Jenckes) and the historical/faith community (Dr. Wyatt Walker).

Where did I acquire the photographs?

I decided to use Flickr Commons and the church photo library, as well as the church photographer's files. Flickr Commons is an online resource. There is a section for "common" use so that one does not have to go through complicated procedures to use photographs. Photographers share them. (Of course, there are those requiring a fee and permissions, which I did not use.) Also the Virginia Youth Advisory Council supplied a few photographs for youth. At that time the group operated under the supervision of the Virginia Department of Social Services. The policy was that youth signed a release form if they did not mind their pictures being used. The agency maintains the release forms. I obtained the images from the VDSS advisory council administrator and VDSS Public Affairs. The Thirty-First Street photographs are maintained and archived by the church photographer. I simply asked to look through his electronic files. If I did not see a picture I described what I was looking for (such as the ordination service with the chain of leaders). In some instances he had images in his personal collection that were applicable to what I needed. His generosity and helpfulness were extremely beneficial. In the case of the images I chose the pictures through a creative process of preparation (as I wrote the script I envisioned what I conceived might portray or illustrate the words), incubation (I put the script aside and looked at pictures from the sources I have mentioned), insight (I chose each picture based on my own visceral hunch), and verification (I asked myself did it feel and look right). This turned out to be a process repeated with each picture. First, I asked myself if each picture was in sync with the unfolding narrative. Second, did it feel right to me when I looked at it—that is, did I get an intuitive sense that it worked? Third, when I played the piece (the audiovisual) in its entirety, did anything jump out as being out of place? I selected pictures that had a collective meaning but that could also be a teaching/renewal moment. For example, many people over forty-five recognize the picture of Emmett Till and know the story of why his mother wanted an open coffin—so that people could see what had been done to her son. Younger people have less of a sense of this. It is a teaching moment in some ways a collective symbol of pain that inspired change. The picture of the lynching as "Strange Fruit," sung by Billy Holiday, is a similar instance. But there are pictures of men and women standing up for what they believed in (appearing as my narration says "we shall not be moved"). There are pictures of the church family appearing toward the end of the piece.

What music should be used?

I decided that the music should be a blend of the rhythmic, lyrics, and the eclectic (traditional gospel, sacred hymns, and the classical traditions). I decided to use two choirs to ground the program in the traditional songs of the church (Thirty-First Street Choir), integrated with the infusion of energy of young people (VCU Black Awakening Choir). I initially approached both VCU and Howard University Gospel Choirs. I submitted a proposal request to each. The challenge was scheduling with Howard. However more and more I was convinced that the intergenerational connection with VCU was important in relationship to Walk into Your Season. This led me to choose VCU. I was familiar with the VCU Black Awakening choir and remembered how they had inspired me as a VCU undergraduate. Their founder lived in Richmond, Virginia. But in order to ascertain if they were what I needed for this program I went to their spring concert. I had communicated with their business manager on the phone and corresponded by email, but I introduced myself to him after the program. I was then convinced that they were the group I wanted. I decided that rather than tell each choir the songs I wanted them to sing, I would ask them to reflect back on the history and songs of empowerment. As they reflected we then decided together what might be appropriate.

What symbol(s) could be conceived as a metaphor(s) of empowerment?

For the first program I decided to use young people who told their stories. For the second, I decided on young Nigel Morris (who opened the program with "Lift Every Voice and Sing") and Miss Felicia

Drake (the "Lady with the Hat"), who entered to a syncopated rhythm and audiovisual backdrop. She then led the choir onto the stage.

Structured Reflection: Focus Groups

Donald Schön (1983) calls for more research on reflective practice. According to Schön, the divergence between research and practice exacerbates the practitioner's "rigor or relevance" dilemma, which in turn tempts practitioners to force practice situations into research derived molds that may be inapplicable (308). Recognizing that practitioners may also become reflective researchers in situations of uniqueness, instability, uncertainty, and conflict, the traditional view is rejected and the relationship between research and practice is recast. In this perspective research is an activity of practitioners. It is undertaken on the spot, triggered by the situation, and linked immediately to action (398). In order to study reflection-in-action, the researcher must learn an art of experiment in which reflection-in-action plays a central part (323).

Heeding Schoen's call for more reflective research I conceive a parallel between the practitioner and the cultural worker. Toward that end focus groups are used in Walk into Your Season. Mihaly Csikszentmihalyi's (1997) conception of creativity informs my decision. He explains that though it seems obvious that creativity is a mental activity occurring inside the heads of certain special people, the assumption is misleading (23). Csikszentmihalyi surmises that if left to individual interpretation alone, all that would be necessary to be creative is one's own inner assurance that what he or she conceives or does is innovative and valuable (24). However, creativity is not so much a question of "what is it"; rather, the question is "where is it" (27).

According to Csikszentmihalyi (1997), creativity is observable in the systematic interrelation of the domain, the field, and the individual person. Domains consist of a set of symbolic rules and

71

procedures embedded in what we call culture. Fields describe the individuals who act as gatekeepers to the domain and decide what should be included in it. When an individual person using the symbols of a given domain (music, literature, engineering, and so on) has a new idea that is selected by the appropriate field for inclusion into the relevant domain, creativity occurs. Occasionally even a new domain is established (27). As such, focus groups allow an assessment regarding creative efficacy and whether success was achieved in Walk into Your Season without relying solely on my own individual interpretation.

Focus groups generate information from homogenous people in a group situation through focused discussion (Krueger and Casey 2009). According to Krueger and Casey, a focus group reveals a distinctive cluster of characteristics. Focus groups (a) involve homogeneous people in a social interaction, (b) collect information from a focused discussion, and (c) are an approach to gathering information that is both inductive and naturalistic. Krueger and Casey describe a focus group study as a carefully planned series of discussions designed to obtain perceptions and explore a defined area of interest in a permissive, nonthreatening environment. The controversy about focus groups resides in the intense involvement between researcher and subject. However, used carefully for a suitable problem in proper context, focus groups are valid (Krueger and Casey 2009).

Krueger and Casey (2009) state that a group has the capacity to become more than the sum of its parts and can possess a synergy that individuals alone do not have. They go on to say that focus groups should be considered when the researcher is (a) looking for the range of ideas or feelings that people should have about something, (b) trying to understand differences in perspectives between groups or categories, (c) looking for the purpose or trying to uncover factors that influence motivation, behavior or opinions, or (d) looking for emergent ideas from the group. The Walk into Your

Season study fit all of these categories. *Walk into Your Season* posits that the success of free space is in empowerment. It is relevant to explore the renewal of the role of free spaces in one setting, and the initiation of free spaces in another. The focus groups inform the exploration of the Walk into Your Season public programs.

Specific questions about the two programs were put to the two focus groups. The questions offered commonality but left enough room for follow-up questions based on the group member's response. The focus group responses inform whether there is substantiation that the values and theories espoused are evident pursuant to cultural work. Even the questions bear explanation since the goal is to gather responses through predetermined questions in order to find the range of opinions, perceptions, feelings, and thinking of people about particular issues. This is not a matter of simply posing open-ended questions (Krueger 1998).

Particular care is warranted because there are characteristics of good focus group questions. Richard Krueger (1998) explains that good focus group questions are good because they sound conversational; they use words the participant would use when talking about the issue; the questions are clear and easy to say; they are usually short and open ended; and they employ the use of one-dimensional questions. The Walk into Your Season focus group participants generated responses to questions related to assessing aspects of the cultural worker, free space and discursive communities, and power and empowerment.

Questions asked to assess aspects of the events in relationship to the cultural worker include the following: What worked well in this program? How effective was the music? How effective was the poetry? How effective was the history? To assess aspects related to free space and discursive communities, respondents considered whether the event was a space that provided or supported pride in who you are? Was it a space in which you were free to express your own understanding of your social position? In order to assess the aspects related to power and empowerment I queried the focus group participants: Did you gain a sense of the history that preceded you to provide better opportunities for your group? Since the time of the event, have you joined with others or acted on your own to provide better opportunities for your group or yourselves?

Krueger and Casey (2000) explain that a focus group must be small enough for everyone to have an opportunity to share insights yet large enough to provide diversity of perceptions. In traditional marketing ten to twelve people are recommended. However, when dealing with complex issues and knowledgeable participants this number is too large. Instead, six to eight participants are recommended. Six people were invited to each Walk into Your Season focus group. Focus Group I (related to Program I) was the social services group which convened on May 14, 2010. Focus Group II (related to Program II) was the church focus group and convened on May 11, 2010. Each group session was recorded and transcribed. Responses from the groups were used in evaluating the efficacy of the cultural worker in the free space settings described. I transcribed the responses myself to become better acquainted with the perceptions.

Walk into Your Season created a space for respective communities to come together around common interests paramount to empowerment. Creativity emerges as a central property that facilitates cohesion and association between related domains integral to cultural work (shared constructions of experience, implicit and explicit patterns, discursive communities, power and empowerment). Constructing a repertoire from the cultural legacy of a group attempts to capture the empowering properties of free spaces while operationalizing the role of the cultural worker. Information generated through focus group discussions is one way of assessing the repertoire, the spaces, and the operationalization of the cultural worker.

Chapter 4: Describing the Walk into Your Season Events

Poets, prophets, and reformers are all picture makers, and this ability is the secret of their power and achievements; they see what ought to be by the reflection of what is and endeavor to remove the contradiction.

—Frederick Douglas (late 1854)

I was leaving the South
To fling myself into the unknown ...
I was taking a part of the South
To transplant in alien soil,
To see if it could grow differently,
If I could drink of new and cool rains,
Bend in strange winds,
Respond to the warmth of other suns
And, perhaps, to bloom.

—Richard Wright

This chapter is a written description of the two Walk into Your Season programs. The program settings are the cornerstone of *Walk into Your Season* because they represent two communities that have allowed me to go beyond a casual glimpse into their experiences. The settings allowed me to explore, observe, learn, question, collaborate, critique, and analyze. I would not have been able to execute this project in the same manner and certainly would not have been able to mine the community resources and develop the concept of the cultural worker in *Walk into Your Season* without the consent and cooperation of these community members. Preparation withstanding, the willingness of the two groups brought the programs I am about to describe to fruition. Each program can be viewed in its entirety at http://www. theculturalworker.com.

Rather than a singular entity (such as a painting or poem) the setting spaces are the canvass, and as the cultural worker I use the cultural legacy of a group to construct a repertoire that includes human dynamics, metaphors, cultural symbols, music, live artists, community members, and poetics, interspersed with original creative work (mini documentaries, poetic inserts, and program scripts). The program order (as printed on the event programs) is represented below followed by a narrative of each event.

Walk into Your Season (Program I) Description
Children's Museum of Richmond
Master Program Template
April 23, 2009
Reception

A reception preceded Program I. At the time I simply believed it to be an appropriate segue from the attendees work day and the program proper which was scheduled to begin at six o'clock in the evening. However, the focus group responses revealed that it evolved into a space within itself and an effective way of creating an atmosphere that supported the work, laid the groundwork for the participant stories, and welcomed the community. The reception was held in the foyer of the Children's Museum. A jazz pianist rendered music. Ushers signaled participants when it was time to move from the foyer into the auditorium. The program unfolded as follows:

Celebrating Foster Care Youth, Workers, and Caring Others
April 23, 2009

Prelude: *Bridge Over Troubled Water*
                   Stanley Scott (guitarist)

Welcome [from the Puppets]

Peyton: Greetings ... The Space Willie Palmer Created

Charismatic Leadership

   Audiovisual

Intellectual Stimulation
         PowerPoint
         Individualized Consideration
                 Voices from the Heart of the City
                 Richmond City Department of Social Services
                 Workers, Youth, and Caring Others
         Inspiration and Motivation
         Grace Notes
         William Prentiss (flutist)
         Free Space for the mime voice ["I'll Trust Him..."]
                 Miss Toni Jones (mime artist)

Narrator/Peyton McCoy:
Willie Palmer had no one to lean on. Willie Palmer's possibilities as well
as his course of action seemed improbable, doomed to fail, unrealistic.
Ummm—unrealistic. But as Joseph Badaracco notes, a realistic David
would have run from Goliath. The American revolutionaries, and

their African and Asian counterparts two centuries later, would never have challenged the British Empire. A handful of American civil rights leaders in the 1950s would never have taken on the legacy of two hundred years of slavery and another century of near-apartheid. Realism too easily leads to patience, delay, or even passivity and defeat. Surely, [not perhaps] surely, [not maybe] surely, [not kinda sorta] surely—our reach should exceed our grasp].

Professor Michael Waltzer of Princeton University, has identified four obligations of morality (a) to protect the life and liberty of its citizens (b) inflict no harm (c) help people avoid man-made and natural disasters (d) assist those who want aid in building better and less repressive political systems. We are defining moral as those issues that produce a net increase in what we associate with la dolce vita—the good life: life, liberty, justice, prosperity, health, and peace of mind. These as opposed to death, repression, lawlessness, poverty, illness and fear. And to get closer—to exceed our grasp— voice must be a part of the equation.

Voice survives even when immediate escape is not an option. The treatment of voice in social movements, notes Dr Richard Couto, suggest a need for broad political change through a voice fostered in organizations, but carried out by individuals who are concerned about the welfare of the group. So perhaps Willie Palmer could not immediately escape his circumstance, but it is encouraging to note that groups restricted by race, class, and gender discrimination regularly develop and express voice in free space.

I don't know if Willie Palmer could have possibly comprehended the dormant possibilities that would spring to life due to the span of his reach and the caring others who extended the capabilities of his grasp, but I can tell you that he transformed the educational landscape for foster care youth. We still hear his voice and that of those in similar circumstances today...come with me and I'll tell you a—no I'll show you a story—from an Independent Living point of view

This program weaves music, narration, and audio visuals to create a space centered upon the independent living history and the people who have experienced it. I created an audio visual presentation to underscore the independent living perspective. At the end of the powerpoint the narrator continues.

Narrator/Peyton McCoy:
All of that started with Willie Palmer. I use to love those books that had pictures with nothing but dots and numbers. And the key was to connect the dots and accompanying numbers. And as one did so the dots were transformed into a picture. Then I liked to color the picture...make something out of nothing. I still believe in connecting dots; my parents taught me the importance of making something out of what appears to be nothing—meaning what superficially seems disjointed and disconnected. So let me try to connect the dots between Palmer, puppets, progress, policy, voice, and justice for all. Back me up Mr. Guitar man.

The guitarist plays softly as the narrator introduces and walks through an audiovisual/ power point.

Narrator/Peyton McCoy:
Reaching beyond the tangible invokes transforming avenues like those you just saw in the audiovisual. However, like each movement of the human arm, many mechanisms are involved in grasping beyond one's reach. The protest, progress, and ensuing policy of the social movement, leadership, *follower-ship*, authority, and power are essential ingredients, integers in any transformation. But the stitches knitting them to one another are not always viewed with adoring eyes. Engaging difference and embracing change can be a challenge. For some it's the difference between a traditional quilter and the avant-garde.

At this point Andrew Martin (Independent Living Social Work Supervisor),Tyler Brackett, Sheena Brown, Diamond Wright (three young people who experienced foster care/ILP) and Dedra Hampton (J. Sargeant Reynolds community College Great Expectations Education Coordinator) spoke. Their individual stories represent the voices of social workers, youth aging out of foster care, and educators who work with youth. The flutist quietly plays songs like Amazing Grace in the background as the speakers tell their stories. Then the narrator continues.

Narrator/P. M.:
So many testimonies are based on the transforming power of free space. The Abrahamic texts are a tapestry of transforming leadership experiences in unexpected places—Abraham, Moses, Joshua. Then down the road there's Ruth meeting Boaz in the grain fields igniting an "overcomer's" testimony through her allegiance to Naomi—a love story to the faithful and a praise song to the widow. Bus seats in Montgomery became a free space for justice. Righteousness rolled like a mighty river and justice flowed like a never ending stream when one man knew how to talk with civility to the no Ds, PhDs, and no pedigrees.

When the songwriter (John Newton) penned this song ("Amazing Grace") a transformation had come about in his life. Another would follow years later. And out of the depths of ugliness, oppression, and pain there came a grace to speak the unspeakable. John Newton's anguish, the ship (the Greyhound), and the angry sea that carried people to slavery became a free space that demonstrated peace—peace in the midst of and in spite of an inner storm and the external predicament. John Newton wrote the words to this hymn in 1772 to describe his feelings about the slave trade after his conversion to Christianity. Purportedly Newton said that his real conversion did not come until much later; just as Willie Palmers impact was not immediately recognized.

The American Cherokee "on the trail of tears" were not always able to bury their dead so this hymn had to suffice. Amazing Grace then is not only a Christian hymn that describes the doctrine of divine grace but it is a favorite of human rights and freedom supporters, both Christian and non-Christian, as they believe John Newton's hymn is his change testimony. John Newton was transformed, Willie Palmer stirred up a transformation, Drs. Wyatt Tee Walker and Martin Luther King and a host of caring others incited a movement— All through the space created (whether a bus seat or the venerable occasion of bestowing the Nobel Prize or the kitchen table when a knock comes at midnight.)

Thro' many dangers, toils and snares,
I have already come;
'Tis grace has brought me safe thus far,
And grace will lead me home.

I have come to believe that hope will get you to first base; faith will carry you to second; free space will open up a passage and usher you onto third; but grace see you home and assure a safe and successful landing.

A fire mist and a planet,
A crystal ball and a cell,
A jellyfish and a saurian, and caves where cavemen dwell—
Then a sense of law and beauty
And a face turned from the clod,
Some of us call it evolution,
And others call it God.

A haze on the far horizon,
The infinite tender sky,
The ripe, rich tint of the cornfields,
And the wild goose sailing high—and all over the upland and the lowland
The charm of the goldenrod,

Some of us call it autumn,
And others call it God.

Like the tides on a crescent sea beach,
When the moon is new and thin,
Into our hearts high yearnings,
Come rolling and surging in—
Come from the mystic ocean
Whose rim no foot has trod,
Some of us call it longing,
And others call it God

A picket frozen on duty,
Mother starved for her brood,
Socrates drinking the hemlock,
And Jesus on the rood—and millions who humble and nameless
The straight hard pathway trod,
Some call it consecration,
[Yet] others [still] call it God (by William Herbert Carruth)

Mime is a unique form of communication. Using the body to interpret music with gestures and facial expressions it speaks without speaking. It is the art of making the audience see what is not there and reaches a wide audience because it breaks language barriers. Miss Toni Jones will take us home tonight as she communicates her belief "I'll Trust You." Ladies and Gentlemen—Mime Artist—Miss Toni Jones

Well they say we don't have to go home. But we must leave here. Good evening!

Dessert was served in the reception area.

Walk into Your Season (Program II)
Celebrating Free Space
Thirty-First Street Baptist Church

Since emancipation, the church was the only organization under the jurisdiction of local African Americans for most of the time. It illustrated an attempt to embrace culture and maintain historical connection. It was (and debatably still is) an example of what Asante (1987) earlier describes as an Afrocentric perspective, an alternative paradigm of social knowledge, a critique of the social sciences. The Walk into Your Season project does not attempt to approve the existence or nonexistence of a core African identity. The project does assert, however, that the African American church as an institution provided a space for decision making and leadership training. It was a space for recounting Biblical narratives of deliverance in spite of suffering, inspiring leaders and participants in the movement for civil rights. It transcended class and position. The program order appears below, followed by a narrativeof the event.

Celebrating Free Space and Cultural Leadership
[Program II] Description
April 26, 2009

Welcome	*Trustee Alice Brooks*
What are we here for?	*Dr. Sharon Campbell*
The Youth Voice	*Mr. Nigel Richardson*
Prayer	*Dr. Janine Hyman*
An Audiovisual Experience	*Free Space and the Church*
31st Street Mime Ministry	*Walk into Your Season*
The Sunday Strut	*Sister Felicia Drake*

The Darrel Rollins Memorial Choir
The VCU Black Awakening Choir
RemarksDr. Larry Preston, Dean/Union I and U
Dr. Morris Henderson, Sr. Pastor

Reception
The Walk into Your Season Project (Program II) Description

Trustee Chairwoman Alice Brooks welcomed just over three hundred attendees to the Thirty-First Street Baptist Church. She thanked the cultural worker for producing the program. It should be noted that by coincidence the deaconate annually celebrates their service and fellowship as leaders in the morning worship service. Walk into Your Season (though held in the evening occurred on the same day, since April 26 was the only available date on the church calendar. In many ways it seemed a continuation of that spirit. Dr. Sharon Curry Campbell, minister of children and youth, described the purpose of the program ("What Are We Here For"), referencing some of the points in the introduction. A young man (Nigel Richardson) representing the youth voice then appeared on the platform. Originally he was to speak the lyrics to the song "Lift Every Voice and Sing," familiar to many as the Negro National Anthem. The lyrics penned by James Weldon Johnson began as a poem in 1899. It was originally written by Johnson for a presentation in celebration of the birthday of Abraham Lincoln. The lyrics were set to music by James Weldon Johnson's brother John. Since the song was originally performed in Jacksonville, Florida, by children it seemed fitting that a child would lead the program proper with his rendition. Master Richardson asked on the day of the program if the cultural leader would mind if he sang the song rather than reciting the lyrics. The audience without provocation came to their feet and joined him. *Nigel Morris began to sing:*

> Lift every voice and sing
> Till earth and heaven ring,
> Ring with the harmonies of Liberty;
> Let our rejoicing rise
> High as the listening skies,

Let it resound loud as the rolling sea.
Sing a song full of the faith that the dark past has taught us,
Sing a song full of the hope that the present has brought us,
Facing the rising sun of our new day begun
Let us march on till victory is won.

Nigel Morris then spoke:
"Lift Every Voice and Sing" by James Weldon Johnson was originally written for a presentation in celebration of the birthday of Abraham Lincoln. It was originally performed in Jacksonville, Florida, by children. Perhaps because the author sensed that the second and third generations would tread an intriguing paradox: awesome opportunity, yet dangerous vulnerability.

Yes—Stony the road we trod,
Yes—Bitter the chastening rod,
Felt in the days when hope unborn had died;
Yet with a steady beat,
Have not our weary feet
Come to the place for which our fathers sighed?
We have come over a way that with tears have been watered,
We have come, treading our path through the blood of the slaughtered,
Out from the gloomy past,
Till now we stand at last
Where the white gleam of our bright star is cast.
My Grandmothers grandfather was a pillar of this church
So I'm here to let you know
The casting of the star shines with bright promise
I'm here to remind you that from generation to generation
We both need each other

I created an audiovisual piece (something akin to a mini documentary) which followed immediately. It began with a dark history (pictures of cloudy skies, an overcast horizon, Emmett Till, the Ku Klux Klan, and a lynching, and ended with a photographs of a discursive community (the Thirty-First Street Church family) and the contemporary jazz infused background music "Oh Happy Day." I am the voice heard on the audiovisual narrating the presentation. The audiovisual narrative follows.

Audiovisual Narrative:
Brooding at the center of the infant earth a catastrophe awaited debut. In the midst of the good and sweet and right, muddy waters and midnight madness sat poised to stand and orchestrate a vitriolic eruption. Let's start at the beginning. At least very near about.

8 ... And while they were out in the field, Cain attacked his brother Abel and killed him. 9 Then the Lord said to Cain, "Where is your brother Able?" "I don't know," he replied. "Am I my brother's keeper?" 10 The Lord said, "What have you done? Listen! Your brother's blood cries out to me from the ground ... which opened its mouth to receive your brother's blood from your hand (Genesis 4:2–10) So we witness the taking of life by the shedding of human blood—the first murder. The notion of taking a life seems morally reprehensible. And many centuries later—the blood cries from the ground the same way.

To a silent backdrop (no background music, just the voice of the narrator) a poem penned by Abel Meerpol [pseudonym Lewis Allan] was recited.

The poem is a staccato juxtaposition of macabre injustice alongside the superficially pastoral southern landscape. As the southern breeze stirs the smell of burning flesh commingling with the sweet scent of magnolia, the poet discerns that the blood dripping appendages dangling from the trees like low lying fruit are bodies. Hence the term "strange fruit." Midway through, the poet reflects on a crop of protruding eyes and twisted mouths before concluding that here swings human fruit for crows to pluck and wind to suck … "here is a strange and bitter crop."[3]

Black people were deemed undeserving of a place or a space of integrity. [At this point the song "Bridge over Troubled Water" is heard and the words "don't trouble the water … still waters run deep" are repeated.] The audiovisual continues as the narrator says:

This poem [Strange Fruit] eventually evolved into the song "Strange Fruit" and was popularized by singer Billie Holiday. It expressed the author's horror at southern lynchings. The "strange fruit" referenced in the poem are the bodies of African American men hanging during a lynching. The chilling lyrics contrast the pastoral southern scenes with the ugliness of racist violence. Some say the dark lyrics were an early seed of a social movement now known as the civil rights movement.

But if we want to understand a social movement as local politics of oppressed people, we have to shift our attention to those who lead movements for change on the local level. It calls for a focus reset away from just national leaders to a crucial, overlooked, and underestimated component of leadership—The people in less visible tiers of leadership—the "plural pantheon" of largely unsung heroes. And many of those people not only emerged in the free spaces created inside (or endemic to) the black church, but also in the black church as a free space. Doug McAdam emphasized the civil rights movement as an insurgency with a context that extended back to reconstruction. During this period of time some African Americans maintained "cognitive liberation" within their organizations despite their oppressed condition. In fact the liberating free spaces of the black church were a shelter from the hailstorm of words and the overcast skies threatening to tear down the house. Words can slice and dice. They can either cut core deep with the healing intent of the surgeon's scalpel or they can dissect the soul like the pirate's

---

3 See full text at www.pbs.org/independentlens/**strangefruit**/film.html.

saber or a mad scientist's machete. There is no prosthesis for an amputated soul.

Come with me as I tell you the story of people, protest, progress, and free space—transformation through space and place, and consecration to cause through perpetual leadership that inspired and transformed. Come with me as I tell you my story.

The audiovisual narrator begins the story with a poem by writer Countee Cullen who was the adopted son of an African Methodist Episcopal preacher. A picture of a mother and her young (probably five or six year old) child appears. The mother holds a newspaper on which the headline reads "Highcourt Bans Desegregation In Public Schools." Cullen was educated at New York University and earned an MA at Harvard. He merged humor, social commentary, and poetry. In the Walk into Your Season *audiovisual a poem is included in which he describes an incident in Baltimore:*

Once riding in old Baltimore,
Heart filled, head-filled with glee,
I saw a Baltimorean
Keep looking straight at me
Now I was eight and very small,
And he was no whit bigger,
And so I smiled, but he poked out
His tongue, and called me, "Nigger,"
I saw the whole of Baltimore
From May until December
Of all the things that happened there
That's all that I remember
[The narration articulates a verse added by the cultural worker:]
I looked at the river as I left Baltimore
And it seemed a repeating theme
For I've known rivers so very well
And marvel at renewal through the redeemed

Sometimes, I felt like a motherless child. I stood on the banks of the Jordan and reminisced the times that I felt like a motherless child.

Narrator then recites a work by Langston Hughes entitled "I've Known Rivers (To W. E. B. Dubois):"

I've known rivers:

I've known rivers ancient as the world and older than the flow of human blood in veins.

My soul has grown deep like the rivers.

I bathed in the Euphrates when dawns were young.

I built my hut near the Congo and it lulled me to sleep.

I looked upon the Nile and raised the pyramids above it.

I heard the singing of the Mississippi when Abe Lincoln went down to New Orleans, and I've seen its muddy bosom turn all golden in the sunset.

I've known rivers;

Ancient, dusty rivers.

My soul has grown deep like the rivers

Margaret Walker's poem "For My People" follows and was selected due to the historical yet quintessential relevance it reflects. The segment used was minimally altered for use in the audiovisual. The narrator, reflecting on Langston Hughes theme on rivers, first says,

But I had one more river to cross. I began a prayer vigil.

[I prayed] For my people everywhere singing their slave songs repeatedly: their dirges and their ditties and their blues and jubilees, praying their prayers nightly to an unknown god, bending their knees humbly to an unseen power;

[I prayed] For my people thronging Forty-Seventh Street in Chicago and Lenox Avenue in New York and Rampart Street in New Orleans, lost disinherited, dispossessed and happy people filling the cabarets and taverns and other people's pockets needing bread and shoes and milk and land and something—something all our own;

[I wanted more] For my people walking blindly spreading joy, losing time being lazy, sleeping when hungry, shouting when burdened, drinking when hopeless, tied and shackled and tangled among ourselves by the unseen creatures who tower over us omnisciently and laugh;

[I took a stand] For my people standing staring trying to fashion a better way from confusion, from hypocrisy and misunderstanding, trying to fashion a world that will hold all the people, all the faces, all the Adams and Eves and their countless generations;

[I stood up for my people] Let a new earth rise. Let another world be born. Let a bloody peace be written in the sky. Let a second generation full of courage issue forth; let a people loving freedom come to growth. Let a beauty full of healing and strength of final clenching be the pulsing in our spirits and our blood. Let the martial songs be written, let the dirges disappear. Let a race of men [and women] now rise and take control.

Then a strange thing happened—very time I thought I was lost my dungeon shook and my chains fell off. I understood Walt Whitman (distinguished for his democratic boldness) as he heard America singing. "I hear America singing," he wrote, "the varied carols I hear."

I am not angry with Mr. Whitman for this description—For I did not detect any condescension in his tone. But I cradled an unspoken question. Who inhabits his American vision? And why did I sense that neither his imagery nor his vantage point included me; did not embrace or reflect me. This in some respects surprised me as Mr. Whitman believed that the mission of his poetry was to put a *person*, a human being—freely, fully, and truly on record. Now this is not to say that the omission was intentional—why it

90

was 1881. Perhaps the omission was unconscious. Nevertheless, I understood all too well the implications of this omission and feel that it is a fitting moment to add another voice to the record. Namely, my own!

I yet be holdin' on but I just wondered where did I fit into the song 'cause I too sing America.

Here the narrator reads the poem "I, too, sing America" with minimal alterations. (Full text at http://www.poetryfoundation.org/poem/177020.) *The poem recalls that in spite of there being no place at the table when company called, and the darker brother having to take his place in the kitchen, he ate well and grew strong and laughed merrily, knowing that another day was forth coming. Tomorrow, when that day comes, nobody will have the audacity to say eat in the kichen. Hughes then prophesies:*

Besides,
They'll see how beautiful [we are]
And be ashamed—[or disturbed, or fearful]
I told Mr. Whitman in absentia
[I thought you knew], [but] I too sing America.

Historically, eating in the kitchen implied a sense of unworthiness, less than, exclusion, underclass. Entertainers traveling in the early- to mid-twentieth century for example (particularly in the south) recollect entertaining for both elite and everyday society, yet sleeping in the same hotels, frequenting the same restaurants, or dining in open spaces was forbidden for Negro citizens. Their appearances and disappearances were controlled by tacit agreement that they were less than—a tacit code that promoted invisibility. Hence they were relegated to the kitchen—where ironically some of the finest meals were made and the best wine was saved for last.

As a the music "Stand" (Sly Stone) begins pictures of the Thirty-First Street community appear in the audio visual at this point.

The table on the other hand signifies a place of inclusion. A democratic witness if you will. For every citizen has a moral right to a place at the table. A voice that can be expressed and that deserves hearing. The implication stretches back to the symbolism of biblical times when the last supper signified a place for all of humanity for the feast at the table. It is significant to note that my muse did not say what events, factors or combination of things will precipitate and facilitate this change of course. Why will tomorrow be different? What will set the stage for this watershed moment? However he has previously indicated that while (segregated) in the kitchen, he grows strong. That growth signifies change and a fertile season that breeds transformation.

The Thirty-First Street Mime Ministry assumed their positions immediately following the audiovisual. Prerecorded music filtered into the sanctuary from the song "Walk into Your Season." The mime ministry is composed of children. Their adult leader is Ms. Nikitta Barrett, who of course does not appear but is always close by. Mime is a unique form of communication. Using the body to interpret music with gestures and facial expressions, it speaks without speaking. It is the art of making the audience feel or see what is not there (historical pain and travail, etc.,) and it reaches a wide audience because it breaks language barriers. As the mime artist performed, pictures flashed on the sanctuary wall depicting seasons (human seasons and nature's seasons).]

Attached to the audiovisual Walk into Your Season *(to facilitate a seamless segue) was music entitled the "Sunday Strut." The "Sunday Strut" by jazz artist Ramsey Lewis is a jazzy piece with a gospel inflection that is at once classy and saturated with confident bounce. At that point Ms. Felicia Drake enters the sanctuary dressed in white (white hat, white suit, gloves) and her commanding presence* typifies "The Sunday Strut." This strut placed in the program was psychosymbolic. It symbolized confidence, somebodyness (reflecting on the historical symbolism of the church as a space where one could be somebody, even if one could not in other dominant spaces), pride, ostensible intrapsychic empowerment, and poetry in motion. As she walked the narrator said:

All week long people have toiled and worked and been subjected to micro aggressions and degradations but come Sunday there seems to be a different attitude. From the rising of the sun until the setting of the same there seems to be a sense that deliverance is available. Style, substance, and service clap hands and synergize voices into a new song that will last all week long. They say they didn't understand Aretha's hat. Well then you must not know about my style and my story.

Ms. Drake continues her strut as pictures are superimposed on the sanctuary wall in this part of the audiovisual including group pictures of the early church, southern leaders meeting on desegregation, Aretha Franklin and her controversial hat worn at the 2009 Presidential Inauguration. The segment culminates as Ms. Drake says, "Come on, Thirty-First Street choir" and leads the choir to their places. The Thirty-First Street choir then sings (a) "I Shall Not Be Moved," (b) "Serving the Lord Will Pay off ..." and (c) "Lord, Lord, Lord, You've Been Good to Me."

Prayer is an essential element of the African American Christian tradition. As the cultural worker I adjusted the program so that the prayer came at the transition point as the Thirty-First Street Choir departed and members of the Virginia Commonwealth University Choir assumed their positions on the platform. This facilitated a seamless transition as the goal was to create a program experience without interruption that emerges as a space for reflection, expression, a modicum of the spontaneity, and improvisation characteristic of free spaces. The researcher (cultural leader) led Dr. Janine Hyman to the platform. Dr. Hyman led the gathering in prayer. The cultural worker then spoke for the first time. The Thirty-First Street Baptist church choir rendered a choral response.

This section carries a corollary theme of deliverance, steadfast hope, and energy. The audiovisual lays the foundation and revisits the despair and injustice. It concludes by conveying a message of hope through a visual collage with a music bed.

> Like a tree that is planted by the water I shall not
> be moved because come what may from day to day
> deliverance is available and in this sanctified space,
> this here place in the African American church, I
> have witnessed the social consciousness o the Black church
> as an institution, and I have experienced the God
> of the universe from generation to generation—to lead me
> and guide
> Me and edify me, Soul's clap hands and sing a new song
> because God is great and God is good; and if God
> doesn't do anything else he's already done more than enough
> meaning what has been done is a firm foundation and a
> charge to keep I now have.
> Deliverance is available and just like a tree so firmly planted
> by the water, I shall not, I shall not, I shall not moved. [Choir
> begins immediately]

I introduced the next choir and noted that the Virginia Commonwealth University Black Awakening Choir's founder was in the audience (Mrs. Arnesto [Ann] Younger). The choir quietly moves into place during this segue.

Peyton McCoy: When all God's Children come together, what a time. A divine coronation, great celebration, soul's salvation, magnificent revelation, what a time.

I'm not talking about a heavenly journey—that time will come for all of us—but every now and then there's a right now on time spirit charged energy infused moment time where a great cloud of witnesses come together to honor one another—serve one another, lift one another. When all God's Children come together—what a time—and welcome to such a time as this.

When all God's children get together what a time. You've come here from the north, south, east, and the west for an occasion ordained to be blessed. When all God's children come together what a time. Sounds so sweet it deserves repeat: what a time, what a time, what a time. And at such a time as this, leadership is evident—we celebrate that. But even more evident is a blessing—the blessing of Abraham. I would tell you about it, but I cannot do it by myself. Are you with me [yeah] can you help me [yeah] what I say. Now help.

The VCU Black Awakening sings "The Blessing of Abraham" and "I Love You, I Really Love You." Their energy is contagious. Remarks were made by Dr. Larry Preston (Academic Dean/Union Institute and University in Cincinnati, Ohio) followed by Dr. Morris Henderson (Senior Pastor of Thirty First Street Baptist Church) and a reception was held in the lower auditorium.

Chapter 5:   Cultural Work and Creativity

Without being bound to the fulfillment of promises, we would never be able to keep our identities; we would be condemned to wander helplessly and without direction in the darkness of each [person's] lonely heart, caught in its contradictions and equivocalities—a darkness which only the light shed over the public realm through the presence of others, who confirm the identity between the one who promises and the one who fulfills, can dispel.

—Hannah Arendt

We train ourselves to respect our feelings and transpose them into a language that can be shared.

—Audre Lorde

While Donald Schön (1983) informs my use of reflective practice in Walk into Your Season, Mihaly Csikszentmihalyi (1997) informs my decision to utilize focus groups because of his conception of creativity. Csikszentmihalyi explains that though it seems obvious that creativity is a mental activity occurring inside the heads of certain special people, the assumption is misleading (23). If creativity is conceived as something original and innovative that has value, says Csikszentmihalyi, just taking a person's own account as the only criterion for the demonstration and existence of creativity is insufficient. Csikszentmihalyi at once poses and responds to the question *where is creativity*, arguing that creativity is a systematic factor falling among the creator, an audience, and keepers of a domain. This means that "personal trait" is not the determining factor in whether a person will be creative. Instead it is whether the innovation they produce is accepted in the domain (28). In the case of Walk into Your Season, the domain and the audience are similar and focus group discussions of the events seem a reasonable step in assessing the achievement of the creative intent of the two events.

The focus group participants were asked a series of structured questions. Focus group responses provide information to ascertain whether success was achieved regarding (a) operationalizing the role of the cultural worker in two settings, (b) exploring cultural work in two settings using tacit knowing, reflective practice, and creativity, and (c) assessing the renewal and initiation of empowerment.

Structured Reflection: Focus Groups

I asked the focus group participants a series of questions designed to assess the events as related to the cultural worker's efficacy in repertoire building because operationalizing the role of the cultural worker draws from this repertoire in creating free spaces. Constructing the repertoire is the building and creation of the language, narrative, poetry, music, and/or tools of a culture. The questions asked in this regard included the following: What worked well in this program? How effective was the music? How effective was the poetry? How effective was the history? Questions were also asked to explore cultural work in two settings. I asked the focus groups: Was the event a space that provided or supported pride in who you are? Was it a space in which you were free to express your own understanding of your social position?

To ascertain and assess aspects of the events as related to the cultural worker on power and empowerment through reflection-in-action, I asked the focus group participants: Did you gain a sense of the history that preceded you to provide better opportunities for your group? Since the time of the event, have you joined with others or acted on your own to provide better opportunities for your group or yourselves?

Assessing How Free Spaces Are Created and the Role of the Cultural Worker is Operationalized

Walk into Your Season conceives that there are sufficient similarities or commonalities in problems and that they are often discerned through tacit knowing. So much so that general principles can be discerned and applied to solve problems through the artistry of reflective practice. For example, the problem situation in the Thirty-First Street discursive community is the renewal of the historical role of free spaces to empower; therefore, tacit knowledge and reflection on the history, narratives, music, images, symbols, traditions, leaders, stories, storytellers, and counter narratives are synthesized and employed in a community setting in order to explore the question. On the other hand, the social service situation considers how to initiate a free space in an emergent community. The repertoire and genres of the established Thirty-First Street community inform the practice and process of discerning the feasibility of initiating an empowering free space in this emergent discursive community. Deriving similarities through Walk into Your Season in order to address these matters simultaneously relies on and builds upon community consciousness and perceptions. These perceptions were obtained through asking the focus group what worked well in this program? How effective was the music? How effective was the poetry? How effective was the history?

Church Group

In asking what worked well we are pondering whether the symbols inserted into the Walk into Your Season program to represent dignity (the woman's hat, sometimes called the crown), oppression (images of Emmett Till and a lynching victim), progress (voting and desegregation signs), disappointment (segregation placard), and hope ("I Have a Dream") still resonate in any way with the Walk into Your Season community. One member provided evidence that the symbols resonated when he responded, "What did it for me was the images." Another commented on the power of music to capture a person's attention, suggesting that a portion of the effectiveness of Walk into Your Season can be attributed to the effective use of music. "To have somebody to tell you and show you what has gone on" was helpful, said a respondent. This seems to say that the cultural worker was perceived as a catalyst and leader in some respects. The focus group members stated that the music, poetry, and history were good saying "everything was excellent." Their response however, seemed to convey that these entities are collectively rather than singularly effective denoting a synergy at work. One element without the others may not have been as effective in this project. An unsolicited remark came from the church group at the end of the session. I asked the group if there was anything else they wanted to share. The group thanked me for bringing the program to their community. The response seems compatible with the notion of the cultural worker as organic catalyst and the relevance of the overall concept in the community.

Social Work Group

While I was an education consultant, counselor, and specialist for social services, I often reflected on ways to mitigate oppressive circumstances of the past, eradicate the stigma associated with foster care, and create a safe place where one could talk and acquire some intrapsychic defenses. How would one know if such an effort was helpful? So in order to ascertain what went well with Walk into Your Season, I asked the focus group. One group member, a social worker by profession, reflected on the beginning of the event. He responded that he felt that the title established the groundwork that facilitated direction early on. "I thought from the beginning you laid a foundation with the title. I could understand and had an idea of what you were going to do," he said. He described inclusion in the collective and respect for ones' individual story as giving "people respect ... having a journey, being able to express oneself in it." Though the question asks *what* went well, the group member responds using the pronoun *you* ("I could understand what you were going to do"). His choice of words conveys recognition of the role of the cultural worker. It also underscores the visibility of the cultural worker. The observation qualifies the efficacy of the cultural worker and perhaps suggests a leadership expectation in cultural work. Other group members pointed to "creativity, "feeling free to express one's story," the "audiovisual," and "creating an atmosphere" as things that went well, all of which are integral to free spaces.

What about collective and intergenerational relevance in this emergent community? The topic or term "intergenerational" appears on six separate occasions in this document. Though it may at first seem a digression, I think it is important to recap the term in the order and context it occurs. The term initially appears in regard to collective sharing and renewal as Nancy Adler reaffirms Kroeber and Kluckhohn's definition of culture and reiterates culture as something older group members pass on to younger group members. Later intergeneration surfaces when Donald Schön submits reflective practice as a means of understanding the professional creativity common to cultural work. For example, when confronted by inconsistent or incompatible demands (e.g., individualism vs. intergenerational sharing), a cultural worker responds by reflective practice about the appreciations they and others bring to the situation. Further on when the topic turns to community conversation and the Walk into Your Season church program, the intergenerational theme manifests though the attendance of a founder of a participating group, the Black Awakening Choir. Then bell hooks recalls a conversation with an acquaintance and their shock, when hooks shares her own desire to purchase a home beside her parent's home. [H]ooks conceives this as an inability to understand the value of sharing intergenerational family life, a mindset that according to hooks is a sign of a looming social problem. Further along, the intergenerational theme arises as I point to my reliance on cultural legacy for scripting the Walk into Your Season programs. I conceived the images narrative and music expressing cultural legacy to at once speak a collective yet individual yet intergenerational language. Finally, the intergenerational connection is mentioned as a factor playing a part in one of my decisions regarding the program participants. In choosing between two of the choirs, both excellent and highly esteemed, I was convinced that the intergenerational connection with VCU was important in relationship to Walk into Your Season. My own matriculation at Virginia Commonwealth University (VCU) and that of others could attest to the inspiring and empowering space the choir had often created. Those of us who had matriculated at VCU recalled how Black Awakening inspired us during our matriculation at what was at that time a predominately Caucasian institution. This meant that the inspiration now spanned two generations.

These aspects of the intergenerational theme shed light on the relevance of Walk into Your Season in an emergent community. The need for older group members to construct ways of transmitting wisdom, reflect on individual identity alongside intergenerational and collective sharing, and to proactively concentrate on decision making with impact outcomes in mind reveals the relevance of empowering practices. A group member's statement relates to intergeneration and is revealing in this regard. "Whether you were two or ninety-two, there was something there so you could relate to the theme." One participant expressed that the young people telling their individual stories was an important part of the program. She also went further saying that they had not been restricted or constrained in terms of how to tell their story so they felt free to tell it. This mirrors the expression of another participant who said that "the young people's speaking was very compelling." This participant then added, "But I also thought the reception was powerful in that we all had an opportunity to just mingle and talk and the young people ... I think it kind of put them at ease and it made it easier for them to tell their stories." The reception was a mixing of generations. When planned, the reception and its accompanying elements (like music) was neither conceived as a free space nor understood as a tool for community building. The focus group, however, saw it as a pivotal and important aspect of the project. The youth telling their stories held what appeared to be reciprocal influence, since some participants said they were encouraged and inspired and more open to sharing their own stories after listening to the youth.

How Does Cultural Work Appear in Two Distinct Discursive Communities?

Cultural expressions are similar to the free spaces described by Sara Evans (2010) in that they help us make sense out of activism that otherwise might appear to come out of nowhere. As such, cultural expressions and free spaces have revealing explanatory power. Each helps us make sense out of culture and is an inextricable part of cultural work. Cultural work reflects, edifies, validates, and exposes shared opportunities for expression.

The expressions of a culture articulate a collective journey, but cultural expressions are also prone to facilitate individual affiliation with the culture. Though often artistic in nature they are also prone to strengthen intrapsychic defenses, such as group solidarity, pride, and traditions (Evans and Boyte 1986). Cultural workers acquaint themselves with cultural expression. They also become familiar with cultural narratives and utilize cultural traditions and/or create new ones. Songs, poems, stories, and other expressions keep culture alive and document the journey. The spirituals for instance were the first artistic gift of Afro-Americans to the world and illustrate existential freedom in action (West 1999a). Willie Palmer's story is an expression that encourages a new generation of youth transitioning from foster care. In this way cultural expressions preserve collective memory but at the same time contrive ways of coping with dominance. For example, historically, cultural expressions in black religion characterized America as depicting Egypt's bondage yet Canaan's milk and honey. They make sense of hidden transcripts (as with Claude McKay's "We Wear the Mask"), and at times they are the hidden transcript (as in the instance of the slave songs).

Yet there are distinctions from setting to setting. Consider, for example, that the social work focus group transcript reveals ten times during the focus group session when laughter erupts, compared to once during the church focus group session. This is not to imply that foster care is a laughing matter, without pain, nor is it to say that laughter is by any means a bad thing. Further, laughter can in part be attributed to personality dynamics. However, I believe the difference regarding laughter in the two groups offers a glimpse into something else. I believe that it is corresponds with the varied healing, reflection, and collective cultural histories that exist from setting to setting. The collective memory of trauma and individual experience contextualized within it is prevalent in the church group, while most members of the social work group do not have such context for their experiences. This simply suggests that the church as an institution reflects upon a longstanding, deeply entrenched, recorded history including rich yet painful stories and images. This stirs the question of whether cultural wounds thwart reflection, cultural renewal, and empowerment. I think not. Instead, cultural work facilitates a counter-narrative in which intrapsychic defenses are engaged, historic contribution, sacrifice, and bravery are recalled, and humor emerges in context. What may be humorous in one setting may be sensitive in another. Nevertheless, the church group still found a humorous moment in the midst of intensity as two respondents volleyed, "[w]e don't have the old folks now [meaning to rely on for cultural guidance] ... that's because we are the old folks [now]." On the other hand, their point is not lost in the moment. The option is no longer available to ask a previous generation to facilitate renewal and tell the story—most of them are gone. The responsibility belongs to those here and now.

Church Group

To assess cultural work in two distinct communities, focus group participants were asked: was the event a space that provided or supported pride in who you are; was it a space in which you were free to express your own understanding of your social position? A focus group respondent comments on the Aretha Franklin hat saying "Some people thought that was a joke. But they didn't understand that the hat, the 'crown,' was a symbol [in the black church]." "During the week she might be a maid or this or that but on Sunday she was a queen." The unspoken affirmation of dignity that unfolds in her statement is unmistakable. The participant talks about the challenges and sacrifices her family made, the sense of community, and a sense of pride.

Another respondent remarked on the "chain" of leaders in a photograph. The photograph appears in the audiovisual. She recalls it as a symbol of strength. She conveys her sense of place in the community as an overcomer as she recalls this image. "When I saw the chain of men I thought about [the late pastor Dr. Darrel Rollins] because I had a phase when I was ready to give up ... but we can't give up on ourselves. We can help somebody. When I share my testimony ... people who had given up themselves are inspired ... [this was a space] where you can open up and share your story just like this."

There are diverse modes of presentation in Walk into Your Season. For example, the focus group participants recall images and symbols in the audiovisual presentation. Thinking about the images and this confluence, a participant discloses that his uneasiness has not gone away. He acknowledges that the recollection of the past is painful for him because he lived it—went through it. Even so, he says, "At least I knew about it so I can understand both the repercussions and the benefits." He continues, "Young people don't have that" now. Another participant interjected that the reason young people don't know is because we didn't tell the story.

Two things happen here, pride in spite of pain and recognition of the power and salience of telling cultural stories. The comments, however, reveal the effectiveness of the history in facilitating reflection, painful as parts may be, and a reminder regarding the need for renewal. The recognition of these symbols exemplifies Kroeber and Kluchohn's (1952) assertion that culture manifests and maintains explicit and implicit behavior acquired and transmitted by symbols. However, the focus group responses also bear witness to the tension between pain and progress and support the premise that the historical role of free space warrants renewal in the discursive community.

Earlier Evans and Boyte (1986) point to black history as demonstrating the way that subversive themes veiled in the dominant culture can be used as resources for struggle, resistance, and self-affirmation. The participant's interest in renewal was embedded in statements like "Every black child should see it" [referring to Walk into Your Season], "I'm afraid my child will encounter racism," "My granddaughter is asking questions," "I'm so afraid we don't know the story," "We need to learn to speak to one another again," and "It was painful but at least I know the story." It seemed to me that the Thirty-First Street focus group was unveiling their tacit understanding of trauma. They convey in their quotes the sense that historical trauma is three dimensional: past, contemporary, and unknown. The participants articulate the need to be empowered to process and metabolize injuries of the past; the need to acquire new tools and positive coping mechanisms that effectively assuage and facilitate counter narratives for combating contemporary assaults;

and a concomitant ongoing need to gain the strength, insight, and resources to fluently navigate the assaults and microaggressions that are yet to come (for surely they will). I hear the past, present, and future in the participant comments. The statements "we need to learn to speak to one another again" and "It was painful but at least I know the story" remind us that it is one thing to recognize pain but yet another to process pain. That, of course, is one of the primary reasons that cultural work is explored.

Social Work Group

The social service program sheds light on a group finding and establishing their community repertoire. The event is an occasion to create a free space but to also reveal the efficacy of the free space. Opportunities for interaction are created and used as an avenue for this community to build its repertoire of cultural expressions. One social worker focus group participant said she realized that it had been just as much a journey for her as the children (meaning youth transitioning from foster care). "Having understood the history [of independent living] I just felt there had been so much accomplished." This social worker met someone whose mother was once at social services with her. The daughter is now doing social work herself, "so of course we felt free to discuss our professions and what we were doing to support the work." These comments convey the pride of progress. Another participant stated that "it was like a reunion for us. Even after the program ... it gave us a chance to continue the conversation, talk with the youth, and offer some encouraging words."

Such statements also indicate that cultural work facilitates opportunities beyond the immediate to build the community. They illustrate shared commitment, group solidarity, and individual interest in the collective. The program title resurfaced as a participant remarked Walk into Your Season granted the opportunity to freely express yourself "whatever your particular season might be ... it gave people the space." The participant believed this freedom of expression was important to the youth who presented their stories, and giving them the "opportunity to do so make[s] a huge impact on their sense of pride and self-esteem." One alumnus of foster care acknowledged that he felt free to disclose his story. Another participant said that a program attendee stated that she had always wanted to share her story and felt encouraged to do so. This goes hand in hand with another participant's feeling that the program title also implies "action" in the word "*Walk*" and "there's actually movement in the space." Still another responded that Walk into Your Season "made me think about my own spirituality." A social work professional stated that the program went beyond just the youth speaking and validated others in attendance. The program used alternative means to consider "authority and space ... which empowered [people] to feel [that] I can ... feel okay about my story. So it was helpful to the professionals there to see this." The statement is important in a discursive community that is building resources since professionals had the opportunity to witness what transpires in cultural work. A focus group participant summarizes, saying, Walk into Your Season was an "opportunity to identify issues that need to change." It was also an opportunity, he said, to "connect these young people with better tools and methods."

Can the Historical Role of Free Spaces Be Renewed or Created?

Questions were put forth to assess the renewal and initiation of the role of free spaces. The focus group participants were asked if they gained a sense of the history that preceded them in order to provide better opportunities for their group. Further, since the time of the event, have you joined with others or acted on your own to provide better opportunities for your group or yourselves?

Church Group

To the question "Did you have a sense of the history?" the participants had several things to say. Here are some of their responses: "Everybody now is so current that we don't know what has gone on."

"This is our history … when we see it we realize it and realize that we ought to be proud of who we are today."

"The photographs of the chain of people signified strength" (note that this photograph is an image of the deaconate linked as a human chain one hand on the shoulder of the person in front signifying their bond and connection).

One participant's comment recalled the hat singer Aretha Franklin wore at the 2009 inaugural, saying "[People] didn't understand that the hat, the 'crown' was a symbol [in the black church]. During the week [a woman] might be a maid or this or that but on Sunday she was a queen."

Another said, "This program [Walk into Your Season] is something that could be shown from generation to generation to generation. Every black child should see it … should learn that Emmett Till's mother wanted the coffin open so people would see and know the story … This was an enlightening experience … it was a free space."

Though the study conceives renewal in a community as important for all members, the focus group participants convey concern about intergenerational pursuits. Focus group participants expressed worry about their children and grandchildren and the next generation's grasp of historical relevance and contextualization in contemporary times. This explains their expression of thanks for bringing Walk into Your Season to the community.

Social Work Group

The sense of history is of course quite different as it relates to the independent living setting. Nevertheless the intergenerational theme emerged in a different way. An intergenerational/relationship matter surfaced in the social work group. A social worker participant commented that she no longer works at the local department in independent living and doesn't do much. She says "at my age there are others who can take this further."

"What do you mean?" says another worker.

"You often serve as a conference youth counselor to forty or fifty youth, you stay connected, and you are here today. That is a lot of work and you didn't have to do it," said the colleague. This former independent living worker appears surprised, as if she realizes that she continues to make a contribution to this community. Perhaps sometimes it takes another member of the community to show or remind us of the difference we are making and that the contribution is valued. This in turn inspires others who are taking notice. It also empowers the person who underestimated their contribution, thinking that it went unnoticed.

Building and identifying with certain symbols, rituals, and traditions was held in esteem by the participants, as were creating new traditions like a Walk into Your Season–type event. Focus group members explain that to them the program title was important. Walk indicates action and that one is free to express oneself regardless of the season in which they live. "Yes," says another, "I think it empowered some of the other youth who were there," not just the three telling their stories. [Here she is also speaking of a few youth who attended the program but had never been in foster care.] One focus group participant is a member of Thirty-First Street but came to the independent living event. She articulates her surprise. She recounts that a young lady who is also a church member came to the event with a friend. "I was encouraged," said the focus group participant. "All these years and I never knew." Now she is keeping up with the young lady who she says wants the opportunity to tell her story. This is interesting yet understandable. It supports what researchers convey. The independent living community needs a host of caring others and consistency from those caring others—being there in and out of season, as one focus group member explains it. There is a stigma, explained a focus group member, that needs to be banished. The interesting point here is that the boundaries of two communities bump up against one another and begin to blend. Also interesting is the number of instances the youth telling their story spoke of spiritual belief, or spiritual grounding.

Wilhelm Dilthey (1985) says all the arts serve to intensify our experience. Many times the arts speak the unspeakable and express the unbearable. For example, it might be hard to express exactly what makes you feel the way you feel. Yet a song like "Amazing Grace" resonates with people and they identify with it. It became a part of the repertoire. This poetic effect, says Wilhelm Dilthey, allows us to pursue the natural process of reflecting on the meaning of our existence—a process that is part of life itself. When a focus group member was asked if any part of Walk into Your Season could be used in their organization he responded.

"Absolutely … this is a wonderful opportunity and way of allowing the youth to share a bit of themselves. Through their own stories …" Using Walk into Your Season in another organization further enhances and facilitates the renewal and initiation of the role of free spaces that empower people.

Observations

I observed several things through the focus groups. The first observation is that the Walk into Your Season focus group responses suggest that cultural work also helps people move beyond the impasse of simply identifying pain in cultural settings toward processing pain. This is exemplified in the focus group interaction and assessed through reflective practice. Pain experienced collectively also has an individual impact. The impact is revealed in an individual's painful memories of verbal slights, career inequities, economic disparity, emotional repercussions, and distress through marginal status assigned to a collective group.

In other words *Walk into Your Season* recognizes and respects cultural legacy, preserves historical relevance while discerning historical lessons learned, considers contemporary relevance and application, and moves beyond painful impasses by identifying and underscoring empowering practices. For example, the retired fireman in the social services focus group took away a clearer realization of his place in the history of resistance and change portrayed in Walk into Your Season. He recalled and articulated the slights, setbacks, and the hurts of being made to feel invisible "like [he] wasn't there." However, when asked how he got through it he responded that that which was intended to distress and diminish him made him better, made him determined, made him explore some options that he otherwise might not have pursued (e.g., going back to school). The pride he demonstrated in feeling that his perseverance helped pave the way for a new conceptualization such that current leadership now embraces diversity in his once segregated firehouse and precinct was evident in this comment and his demeanor. "I am a part of the history you are talking about," he said. What this focus group member articulates underscores Asante's conception of transforming alienation into pride.

The second observation is that cultural productions like Walk into Your Season promote group consciousness and in the process also make groups sensitive to the existence of challenges that confront other cultural groups. This provides a group the opportunity to review their actions, inactions, oversights, and misconceptions in light of revelations from their own collective and individual pain processing. For example, a social work focus group participant was surprised to learn that a member her own church congregation had a foster care story that she wanted to tell but was afraid to do so. This focus group member revealed that one of her young church members attended the Walk into Your Season social work program to support a young person who was performing. The youth was surprised to see that there were young people speaking and sharing who had been through foster care experiences. The young lady shared with the focus group member that as a result, she felt that she could tell her story and seek people for support. Normally this focus group member would not have been at the social work event. However, knowing that she would not be attending her preferred event (the church event) due to a scheduling conflict, she wanted to gain an understanding of what the concept cultural work was about. Her attendance (and that of others either in similar scheduling predicaments or attending by coincidence) sheds light on the malleable nature of community boundaries. This blurring of boundaries is somewhat intriguing. People began to talk who normally would not have done so. Interest in another community is initiated and opportunities to learn more, serve as supportive community members and advocates, widen the circle of support, and benefit from reciprocal learning are manifested. The focus group member's comments provide further evidence regarding the renewal of the historical role of free spaces.

The third observation is that the Walk into Your Season focus groups were an opportunity to test the group memory and effectiveness of the settings, obtain lasting impressions, collect suggestions for improvement, and explore windows of opportunity and possibilities that I either overlooked or perceived differently. Much to my surprise, cultural symbols were readily recalled. For example, in the church program focus group a lively discussion of Aretha Franklin's hat recounted the traditional role and story of the hat for African American Women. The hat is more than an emblem of style or fashion adoration, said the focus group member. It is also a historical representation of pride. The focus group member explains that as documented in the play *Crowns* the hat was a symbol of dignity and somebodyness. Women who couldn't take their rightful place in any other setting at the time could do so on Sunday mornings fully regaled in their crowns.

A social service focus group participant recalled the Willie Palmer story. She traced and connected it to her own work. The group member recalled a time when people were "closing cases left and right because there were no services for youth transitioning from foster care." The focus group member reveals her use of the Palmer story believing early on that it was an empowering catalyst. She articulates pride in having had the opportunity to bring value to an unfortunate story. The Palmer story continues to empower, however, the striking factor here is the focus group member's recollection, connection (of personal effort and experience to contemporary circumstance), and ability to recall nascent opportunities to create resources using story and symbol (the Palmer story) in an empowering context.

The fourth observation is that Walk into Your Season had some pleasant though unexpected surprises, not just in the mixing of communities but also due to the unanticipated, untapped spaces and opportunities therein. For example, focus group members identified the program reception as a space. As the cultural leader, I did not initially conceive it as such. A focus group participant remarked, "Even before the program there was a kind of ... space in the reception area ... [and] interaction among people ... Even after the program [cake in reception area] it gave us a chance to continue the conversation, talk with the youth, and offer some encouraging words ... I think that when you walk into your season you feel free to express yourself."

While I conceived the reception as a relevant, empowering space, the impact may never have been fully revealed had the interpretation been left solely to my own analysis. However, the cultural worker's principles produced through the work in this study depicts the cultural worker as a learner-collaborator. This learner-collaborator relationship is revealed in this illustration. Though unanticipated, the focus group reflects and goes on to interpret and identify the reception as a space, and then gave their reasons for viewing it as such.

The fifth observation is that Walk into Your Season used language to inform, inspire, and invite critical reflection. The use of art forms as language in cultural work is multifaceted. A focus group member remarked, for example, that when "you put something to music it grabs your attention ... a song on the radio will grab your attention and bring back memories." Language then might entail traditional cultural genres (sermons, spirituals, and hymns) that rekindle collective memory and garner strength to endure, borrowed genres (the women's movement effectively adapted language, tools, and songs from the civil rights movement), or the creation of new genres (hip hop, spoken word, social networks). The discourse is often expressed and revealed through these genres.

Chapter 6: Conclusion

It may be a mistake to mix old and new wines, but old and new wisdom mix admirably.

—Bertolt Brecht

Cultural work develops and refines generalized theoretical understandings of social processes such as race or class subordination or youth transitioning from foster care. The purpose of *Walk into Your Season* is seeking to understand and make sense of complex social worlds demonstrated in discursive communities of which we are only a part (but nevertheless a part).

What Makes Cultural Work Effective

Walk into Your Season is effective due to the synergy of tacit knowledge and reflective practice, and creativity through repertoire construction to sustain, augment, and create discursive communities. *Walk into Your Season* examines the role of the cultural worker and four related factors, (a) cultural work, (b) free space, (c), discursive communities, and (d) empowerment. It explores the cultural worker's examination of renewing the role of free spaces to a new generation in a discursive community that empowers people and initiating it in a new community.

Observations manifested through the Walk into Your Season project illuminate the understanding of cultural work in discursive communities. It is fair to say from the onset that the most obvious yet often understated contributor to the effectiveness of cultural work is the existence or discernment of common factors or shared experiences that find expression in the free spaces of the discursive community. In the Walk into Your Season Thirty-First Street setting a common binder is the black church as an institution and conduit for the individual and collective historical experiences that unfold in a creative repertoire. In the case of the Department of Social Services, foster care is the common connector. However, unlike the church, the historical foundation for building the foster care discursive community is inchoate. Renewal in the former offers insight for the latter. That is, the progress embedded in the repertoire of the black church as an institution are instructive in understanding and coming to grips with community building in the foster care setting.

The conditions paramount to *Walk into Your Season* illustrate the paradoxical role of the cultural worker. A cultural worker is a cultural critic yet consumer, a community catalyst and community learner/collaborator, a researcher yet a community insider. These conditions inform our understanding of cultural work revealing that (1) the cultural worker is a researcher and a member of the social world being studied who constructs a creative repertoire through the cultural legacy of a community; (2) as a member, this cultural worker has a dual role as an insider of sorts in the social world under study and as a researcher with inherent responsibilities in that world; (3) dual membership exposes the enhanced visibility of the cultural worker's self and necessitates committed ethical responsibility to both craft and community; (4) the cultural worker is aware of the reciprocal influence between cultural workers and the discursive community and informants such as focus group members; (5) the dialogue with informants extends beyond self-interest and introspection; (6) creativity unfolds on two dimensions—in the artistry demonstrated through the process of reflective practice as well as in the emergent assembly of creative products (poetry, music, essays, audiovisuals, etc.); (7) empowerment is expressed by members of the community rather than left solely to the interpretation of detached observers or the self-interests of the cultural worker; and (8) commitment to theoretical and empirical analysis and rigor through reflective practice is ongoing. Rigor is asserted through reflective practice. Alongside these conditions, tacit knowledge emerges as an important aspect of cultural work. These conditions and the cultural work of Walk into Your Season allow the manifestation of principles that I believe to be germane to the cultural worker.

The Principles of a Cultural Worker

Through the discussion of cultural work and the themes relevant to it in the literature review, cultural artistry emerges as a central property that facilitates cohesion and association between related domains integral to cultural work (shared constructions of experience, implicit and explicit patterns, discursive communities, power and empowerment). A template that illustrates the connection may be beneficial to developing the concept.

As a result of the focus group responses obtained through structured reflection, I developed a template (resembling a protocol in some respects) called *The Principles of a Cultural Worker.* The template (a) owes much to the researchers whose work is described in the literature review and identified in the methods section, (b) is informed and edified by the work of Douglas Perkins, and (c) incorporates adaptations from Kenneth Maton and Deborah Salem's efforts to identify central characteristics common to empowering settings. However, "The Principles of a Cultural Worker" are clearly an outgrowth of the emergent work of Walk into Your Season.

The principles are a framework that encapsulates the characteristics of a cultural worker so that the cultural worker can then proceed with cultural work that applies common principles to cultural work in diverse communities. Just as Kroeber and Kluckhohn (1952) synthesized definitions to achieve a common working definition of culture, the principles allow for synthesis, common characteristics of the cultural worker, empowering settings, and cultural work derived from the research in order to format a template. The reflective process is embedded in the framework. This framework evolves through the cultural work put forth in the two settings described. It establishes a tool by which to gauge, identify, and assess existing empowering settings in order to facilitate outcomes. It serves as a structure to identify those settings, which are yet to be defined. *Walk into Your Season* also conceives the Principles of a Cultural Worker as a template others (leaders, organizers, groups, and organizations) might follow to impose order and constancy . The principles are as follows:

1. Cultural workers engage in reflection-in-action and operate as catalysts. Though often connected or holding interests in particular indigenous traditions, critical catalysts are very much engaged in rigor, the life of the mind, writing, reading, and so on. Cultural workers acknowledge the interplay of leadership, order, and organization in helping others to help themselves.

2. Cultural workers seek and use personal, organizational, and community narratives and other qualitative knowledge about real-world empowering processes to facilitate and sustain empowering settings.

3. Cultural workers are conscious *of* and thus pay attention *to* different levels of empowerment (i.e., individual and collective) because people find individual identity and affirmation, and group consciousness.

4. Cultural workers recognize the paradoxes of empowerment, such as (a) people's needs for both individual and community identity within empowering spaces; (b) simultaneously acknowledging personal, collective, and spiritual control domains; (b) the paradoxical requirements of culture

work such as order, and organization in helping others to help themselves; (c) the need for change yet stability; (d) the personal and organizational benefits of greater empowerment along with and in spite of its risks and challenges; (e) professionalism with an ethic of care; and (f) an approach to theory and research on empowerment that allows for both deductive and inductive logic.

5. Cultural workers utilize a mindset that smaller (as in the Walk into Your Season settings) is sometimes better.

6. Cultural workers focus on empowering behaviors such as individual participation in the discursive community.

7. Cultural workers embrace and exemplify the role of learner-collaborators rather than strictly scientists and as a co-learner-collaborator with the community, exemplify the antithesis of the detached or passive leader, expert, or recipient.

8. Cultural workers identify those who can make or affect empowering policies and practices and cultivate information channels with multiple dimensional audiences.

9. Cultural workers are proactive from agenda formation and program implementation to review and reflection.

10. Cultural workers facilitate, contribute to, and create opportunities to sustain discursive communities through empowering settings (programs, performances, organizations, environments), which exemplify certain characteristics. The cultural worker strives to cultivate, contribute to, identify, and sustain such settings through their efforts in cultural work. Cultural work then endeavors to facilitate empowering settings identifiable through four common characteristics:

   a. Leadership that is inspirational, visionary, shared, and committed to the community

   b. Resource cultivation that activates individual and collective resources and participation

c. A supportive group climate marked by shared events, celebrations, and ritual

d. A belief system that fosters critical awareness, transcends self-concern, includes individual, organizational, and community narratives, and focuses on member's strengths

Shortcomings of the Methodology

All methodologies have shortcomings. Cultural work is no different in that regard. Effective cultural workers possess awareness and endeavor to provide safeguards against potential vulnerabilities residing in cultural work. Any propensity to focus excessively on self-interests rather than the discursive community, overemphasis on narrating the story to the exclusion of cultural interpretation and analysis, or relying solely on personal memory and recollection as resources, prohibits and/or interferes with the renewal and initiation of resources in discursive communities.

Even so there are clear shortcomings, since the very same properties that make cultural work effective on the one hand also pose limitations on the other. For starters, most researchers do not find their research interests as deeply entwined with personal interest(s) and lives as cultural work requires. Just as any competent researcher must acquire the ability to use various research skills, cultural workers must do likewise. They must become adept in questioning and thus work on fluency in reflective practice, analysis, focus groups, and so on. They must develop the skill and insight to discern those occasions, settings, and issues when cultural work is likely to prove more productive than other types of research. Conversely, they must be aware of moments when cultural work is not appropriate or would be a hindrance to outcomes rather than an asset based on the research objective.

Second, the cultural worker has a simultaneous role as a researcher and as a member or an individual holding vested interest(s) in the discursive community being studied. This can prove counterproductive and limiting if the cultural worker leans or gives way to self-indulgence or self-aggrandizement. Cultural work is not about the cultural worker's agenda. It is about being in tune to the issues, needs, and agenda expressed by the community while constructing a repertoire facilitating the space. The dialogue that ensues through reflective practice and the focus group is a formidable antidote for blind self-indulgence and constrains self-absorption. However, cultural work is qualitative. Due to the human dynamic, even though safeguards are imposed, complete circumvention cannot be guaranteed.

Third, even in the safeguards there is inherent risk in cultural work. People forget things. Individual memory is sometimes flawed and community memory to some degree evolves from individual recollection. For that reason, overstating, exaggerating, misinterpreting, or misrepresenting experiences and events, even if unintentionally, are inherently a possibility. The rigor of reflective practice mitigates these risks so that unintended consequences do not disproportionately outweigh the advantages and opportunities of cultural work.

Fourth, cultural work like the Walk into Your Season programs are often onetime events. This means that results are not gauged over time. In order to assess cultural work as viable for the long haul, consistency must be established. In so doing, empowering settings are not assumed to come about through luck, accident, occasional happenstance, or just appear as if by magic out of nowhere.

Fifth, participation in cultural work can be hard to negotiate. Youth members of Walk into Your Season were not available to participate in the focus groups. This is endemic to this community and mirrors the accessibility that is often confronted by social workers and concerned others as youth transition from care. (It is also an inevitability of early adulthood when college, postsecondary training, military, and responsibilities limit availability.) A onetime event cannot eradicate an entrenched social reality. Moving from place to place out of necessity is often due to the lack of stability that comes from the absence of family connections. A fixed stable residence can be elusive. As a result difficulties in locating older youth are commonplace. On the other hand, a onetime event can indeed initiate and progress the conversation. It can give voice to experience. This is perhaps all the more reason to explore empowering settings and the building, long term maintenance, and transfer of resources in discursive communities which foster individual and collective nurturing.

Finally, in the case of Walk into Your Season, choices and timing were pivotal yet sometimes beyond my control. I needed the buy-in from participants. Some decisions regarding things like affordable space, venues conducive to the discursive communities, youth availability, availability of the preferred venues, and scheduling conflicts with the preferred dates were outside of my control and influence. However, the flip side of the coin is that in the instance of Walk into Your Season and for this type of research, had I waited any longer there is no telling whether the events would have ever been executed in these settings by this cultural worker. A rich opportunity would have been lost had the events not been conducted. There may not have been a starting point on which to construct this repertoire.

Areas for Further Research

"Principles of a Cultural Worker" emerge from the Walk into Your Season study and offer a template to consider in erecting, sustaining, and analyzing empowering settings. However, development of a strategic means of quantifying and measuring the effectiveness of the settings and the quantifying demonstrated outcomes of those settings requires further research. Also, quantifying the effectiveness of the characteristics and properties of the empowered setting as depicted in the "Principles of a Cultural Worker" should be pursued.

Cultural Work and Social Networks

Assessing the application of cultural work to other settings and assessing the effectiveness in contemporary yet evolving entities like Facebook, Twitter, Pinterest, and yet-to-be-established social media should be contemplated and pursued. For example, will these entities without the face-to-face element identified as characteristic of the discursive community still benefit from cultural work? If so, who are the identifiable leaders, and what are the identifiable institutions, roles, and the characteristics of each? Are identifiable leaders and institutions needed? Who is the cultural worker in such settings, or are there multiple cultural workers and are they needed? And what does a virtual relationship mean for cultural work in the world of social networks? How is the repertoire constructed? What are some of the untapped means through which the creativity of cultural work might express itself in emergent social media? And what are some opportunities that serve the common good? Does free space in cyberspace exist, or is it even attainable? If attainable, how does the texture of the virtual space change when everyone is looking? These are questions beyond the scope of this research, yet they are necessary questions.

Earlier I discussed the Walk into Your Season venues in terms of Gaventa and Pettit's (2010) power cube. The black church represents a claimed/created space and the children's museum represents an invited space. Each venue represents a local place. This power cube also illustrates the forms of hidden and invisible power within the discursive communities explored. The Gaventa and Pettit power cube and the Cultural Worker's Protocol might also be used in developing exercises that explore the diverse types of spaces, places, dimensions and their inter-relatedness alongside the utilization of the principles. Such exercises would at the same time stimulate discussion about cultural work. A work book might be developed that includes such exercises that facilitate discussions in discursive communities.

Cultural Work, Courage, and Reflection-in-Activism

Creativity, free spaces, discursive communities, tacit knowledge, and reflective practice are ingredients of Walk into Your Season that need further study. The cultural work of Walk into Your Season is relevant to problem solving, diversity, social malaise, and community progress in the manifold dimensions (local, national, global and so on) that Gaventa and Pettit (2010) express. The diversification of postmodern society necessitates manifold but effective means of grappling with familiar problems and the new challenges that they bring. Cultural workers support individual and collective empowerment and strive for edification of the common good through empowering settings.

Consider a group of ordinary women in Liberia led by Leymah Gbowee, a social worker. Never imagining that their efforts would empower people around the globe, the women simply came together to pray for peace. In fact they came together to "Pray the Devil Back to Hell," a phrase that became the title of a film produced by Abigail Disney that documents a peace movement. The movement started with praying and singing in a fish market. For fifteen years, Liberia was gripped by civil war between the government of the corrupt and ruthless Charles Taylor, as well as warlords battling to overthrow him. More than two hundred thousand people had been killed, and one out of three were made homeless. Gbowee was only seventeen when war first came to Monrovia. She says that she turned from a child into a woman in a matter of hours. As the war went on it seemed that her dream of education and college had dissolved in an instant. She was bitter and disappointed and shunned social and political involvement. She trained as a trauma counselor and worked with the ex-child soldiers of Taylor's army. The more she worked with them, the more she came to see that they too were victims. Leymah Gbowee and her countrywomen reached desperation. She came to see that it would be up to the citizens of Liberia, especially its women, to bring the country back from the insanity of civil war. Gbowee joined the Women in Peacebuilding Network (WIPNET). Then she brought all the women of the Christian churches together into a group called the Christian Women's Initiative, which issued a series of calls for peace. Soon a coalition with the women in the Muslim organizations in Monrovia was formed and eventually Liberian Mass Action for Peace came into being. They decided to try to put a stop to the fighting. They took to the streets armed with just a white T-shirt, knowing they could very well be beaten and killed. But they evolved into a sea of white T-shirts. They became "the market women," cajoling the fighting men and employing an old tactic, so old it was once used by the women of ancient Greece: no peace, no sex.

Dressed in white to symbolize peace, numbering in the thousands, and armed only with white T-shirts and the courage of their convictions, the women became a political force against violence and against their government. They demanded a resolution to the country's civil war. The at once poignant and powerful title comes from Gbowee's statement about then President Charles Taylor and the rebels. Both sides were supposedly religious. The rebels frequented mosques, while Taylor was a devout Christian who, according to Gbowee, could "pray the devil out of hell." It was therefore the responsibility of the women in this interfaith coalition to pray the devil (of war) right back to hell. And perhaps they did. Charles Taylor was toppled from power and banished from Liberia. The country then elected a new president, the first woman head of state in Africa, Ellen Johnson-Sirleaf.[4]

---

4 See more http://africanhistory.about.com/od/liberia/p/Sirleaf.htm

It is not a stretch of any sort to consider Gbowee a cultural worker who exemplifies the principles. As we observe her actions and efforts, we wonder not only how her effectiveness is continued in a discursive community but also how it can create other discursive communities. It is also important to remember that her effective utilization of resources to create a space facilitated the entrance of another leader whose gifts otherwise may not have been utilized and supported. Whether that leader is a cultural leader or not is beyond the boundaries of this study. However, Gbowee's work bears testament to a committed cultural worker who, it appears, was instrumental in facilitating empowering practices. Music, verse, and metaphor were evident (as were shock, empathy, and action) and the deliberate, strategic yet appropriately spontaneous creativity allowed community building, healing, identity, and cultural transmission, wisdom transmission, and the already mentioned social capital.

Cultural workers can be ordinary people, as was Leymah Gbowee, who, undeterred by immensity, accomplished the extraordinary. The space carved by these workers is encouraging due to their ability to achieve the psychopolitical through the effective utilization of resources in their repertoire to advance and empower. Little becomes much (a song, poem, or lyric articulating pent up emotion and thus inciting a movement) and much (insurmountable odds) becomes less. This is not to romanticize the worker's challenges as "their efforts require hard work and creativity" (Couto and Gutherie 1999, 1).

This creativity and hard work captures the prevailing circumstance and spirit of Florence Reece. Reece was subjected to the ransacking of her home due to her husband's (Sam Reece) involvement in organizing coal miners into a labor union, the United Mine workers of America. In spite of violent reprisals, she transformed the memory of a fearful night into the lyrics of the song "Which Side Are You On?" which spoke to a dichotomous society, the affluent and the working people, the company and the miners. It was the sheriff and the deputies sent by the coal company (enforcing the wishes of the company as law) who ransacked the home of Sam and Florence Reece and their seven children. So Florence Reece posed a question that brought miners and their caring others face to face with a choice: collective action for improvement or resignation to unbearable conditions and company repression supported and enforced by local authorities—the union or the coal company and the sheriff (Couto and Gutherie 1999). Neutrality was not an option. The gearshift of a moving train cannot remain in neutral.

Conclusion

Cultural work considers the historical role of free spaces yet the multidimensions and intricacies of contemporary problems. It questions and tests the role and application of artistry in sustaining communities yet contextualizes and considers historical resources.

The cultural work of *Walk into Your Season* embraces rigor as a necessary part of any research process. There is no substitute for knowing and relentlessly pursuing one's craft. Pairing and applying the appropriate tool and/or set of tools for the right research pursuit is tantamount to possessing the right surgical tools for exploratory surgery that has life-enhancing potential due to its revelations. Reflective practice brings rigor and the appropriate tools to cultural work and the ultimate goal of empowerment.

Walk into Your Season explores reflective practice through experimenting with renewal in the free space of one discursive community and initiation of free space in another—the renewal of a liberation tradition in one community and the initiation of the tradition in another. The movie Drumline (2002) is a contemporary illustration of Bertolt Brecht's conception of mixing the old and the new that begins this chapter. In the movie, prior to starting rehearsals for the culminating event the band director makes a statement to the band. "We're going to try something new this year—a little bit of the old and a little bit of the new—old school and new." And that's the way it was, is, and shall be in the case of this cultural worker—walking into a new season with an illuminating appreciation of the old.

References

American Psychological Association. 1993. *Guidelines for Providers of Psychological Services to Ethnic, Linguistic, and Culturally Diverse Populations.* American Psychologist.

AAPA, ABPsi, NLPA, and SIP. 2003. Council of National Psychological Associations for the Advancement of Ethnic Interests. *Psychological Treatment of Ethnic Minority Populations.* Washington, DC: Association of Black Psychologists.

Adler, N. 2008. *International Dimensions of Organizational Behavior.* Boston: Kent.

Adler, P., and P. Adler. 1987. *Membership Roles in Field Research.* Newbury Park, CA: Sage.

Anderson, L. 2006. Analytic Autoethnography. *Journal of Contemporary Ethnography,* 373–395.

Appiah, A. 1992. *In My Father's House: Africa in the Philosophy of Culture.* New York: Oxford University Press.

Appiah, A. 1996. "Race, Culture, Identity: Misunderstood Connections." In A. Appiah, and A. Gutman, eds., *Color Conscious: The Political Morality of Race,* 26. Princeton: Princeton University Press.

Asante, M. 1987. "The Search for an Afrocentric Method." In M. Asante, *The Afrocentric Idea,* 159–181. Philadelphia: Temple University Press.

Baldwin, J. 1967. *The Creative Process.* New York: Ridge Press.

Berger, P., and R. Neuhaus. 1977. *To Empower People: The Role of Mediating Structures in Public Policy Research.* Washington D.C.: American Enterprise Institute for Public Policy.

Boyte, H. 1984. *Community Is Possible: Repairing the Roots of America*. New York: Harper and Rowe.

Brown, E. 1992. "What Has Happened Here: The Politics of Difference in Women's History and Feminist Politics," *Feminist Studies* 18 (2): 295–313.

Burke, K. 1941. *The Philosophy of Literary Form*. Berkley: University of California Press.

Calhoun, C. 1980. "Community: Toward a Variable Conceptualization for Comparativeresearch." *Social History* 5: 105–129.

Carson, C. 1980. *The Landmark Speeches of Martin Luther King, Jr.* New York: IPM/Warner Books.

Chapman, A., ed. 1972. *New Black Voices*. New York: New American Library.

Csikszentmihalyi, M. 1997. *Creativity: Flow and the Psychology of Discovery and Invention*. New York: Harper Perennial.

Christian, B. 1988 (spring). "The Race for Theory," *Feminist Studies* 14 (1): 70.

Cone, J. 1970. *A Black Theology of Liberation*. Philadelphia: Lippincott.

Cone, J. 1986. *My Soul Looks Back*. Maryknoll: Orbis Books.

Couto, R. 1993. "Narrative, Free Space, and Political Leadership in Social Movements," *The Journal of Politics* 55: 57–79.

Couto, R. A. 2007. "Leadership As Effective Narratives of Adaptive Work." In R. A. Couto, ed., *Reflections on Leadership*, 163–184. Lanham, MD: University Press of America.

Couto, R., and C. Gutherie 1999. *Making Democracy Work Better*. Chapel Hill: University of North Carolina Press.

Douglas, F. 1864. Frederick Douglas papers. Library of Congress.

Eagleton, T. 1976. *Marxism and Literary Critism*. Berkeley: University of California Press.

Evans, S. 2010. "Free Spaces." In R. Couto, ed., *Political and Civic Leadership: A Reference Handbook* (vol. 1), 359–364. Thousand Oaks: Sage.

Evans, S., and H. Boyte. 1986. *Free Spaces*. New York: Harper and Row.

Foucault, M. 1973. *The Birth of the Clinic: An Archaeology of Medical Perception*. Translated by A. Smith. New York: Pantheon Books.

Foucault, M. 1980. *Power/Knowledge: Selected Interviews and Other Writings*. New York: Pantheon Books.

Foucault, M. 1984a. "The Body of the Condemned." In P. Rabinow, ed., *The Foucault Reader*, 170–184. New York: Pantheon Books.

Foucault, M. 1984b. "Truth and Power." In P. Rabinow, ed., *The Foucault reader*, 51–75. New York: Pantheon Books.

Fraser, N. 1990. "Rethinking the Public Sphere: A Contribution to the Critique of Actually Existing Democracy," *Social Text* 25 (26): 56–80.

Freire, P., and A. Faundez. 1989. *Learning to Question: A Pedagogy of Liberation*. New York: Continuum.

Gardner, H., and E. Laskin. 1995. *Leadingminds: An Anatomy of Leadership*. New York: HarperCollins.

Gaventa, J., and J. Pettit. 2010. "Power and Participation." In R. Couto, ed., *Political and Civic Leadership: A Reference Handbook* (vol. 1), 513–522. Thousand Oaks: Sage.

Gilliam, K. 2000. "We Take It from Where We Need It: A Portraiture Approach to Understanding Social Movement through the Power of Story and Storytelling Leadership." PhD dissertation. Antioch University. Ohio, United States. Retrieved May 20, 2010, from Dissertations and Theses: Full Text. (Publication No. AAT 3252324).

Golden, E. 2010. "Creativity and Innovation." In R. Couto, ed., *Political and Civic Leadership*, 926–937. Thousand Oaks: Sage.

Goodwin, J., and J. Jasper. 2009. *The Social Movements Reader: Cases and Concepts*, 2nd ed. J. Goodwin and J. Jasper, eds. United Kingdom: Wiley-Blackwell.

Gouldner, A. 1979. *The Future of the Intellectuals and the Rise of the New Class.* New York: Seabury.

Gutierrez, L., and R. Ortega. 1991. "Developing Methods to Empower Latinos: The Importance of Groups," *Social Work with Groups* 14: 23–43.

Habermas, J. 1991. *The Structural Transformation of the Public Sphere.* Translated by T. Burger. Cambridge: MIT Press.

Hansen, N., F. Pepitone-Arreola-Rockwell, and A. Greene. 2000. "Multicultural Competence Criteria and Case Examples," *Professional Psychology: Research and Practice* 31 (6): 652–660.

Harding, S. 2006. *Science and social inequality: Feminist and postcolonial issues.* Chicago: University of Illinois.

Hayward, C. R. 1998. "De-facing Power," *Polity* 31: 1–22.

hooks, b., and C. West. 1991a. "bell hooks interviewed by Cornel West." In b. hooks and C. West, *Breaking Bread: Insurgent Black Intellectual Life,* 65–91. Cambridge: South End Press.

hooks, b., and C. West. 1991b. *Breaking Bread: Insurgent Black Intellectual Life.* Cambridge: South End Press.

hooks, b., and C. West. 1991c. "Cornel West interviewed by bell hooks." In b. hooks and C. West, *Breaking Bread: Insurgent Black Intellectual Life,* 27–58. Cambridge: South End Press.

Jackson. L. 2000. "The New Multiculturalism and Psychodynamic Theory: Psychodynamic Psychotherapy and Afrcan American Women." In L. Jackson and B. Greene, *Psychotherapy with Afrcan American Women: Innovations in Psychodynamic Perspectives and Practice,* 1–15. New York: Guilford Press.

Jasper, J. 1997. *The Art of Protest: Culture, Biography, and Creativity in Social Movements.* Chicago: University of Chicago Press.

Kelly, G. 1955, 1995. *The Psychology of Personal Constructs* (vol. 1 and 2). New York: W. W. Norton.

Kroeber, A., and C. Kluckhorn. 1952. *Culture: A Critical Review of Concepts and Definitions.* Cambridge: The Museum.

Krueger, R. 1998. *Focus Group Kit*. In D. Morgan and R. Krueger, eds., *Focus Group Kit*. Thousand Oaks: Sage.

Krueger, R., and M. Casey. 2000, 2009. *Focus Groups: A Practical Guide for Applied Research.* Thousand Oaks: Sage.

Lorde, A. 1984. "Age, Race, Class, and Sex: Women Redefining Difference." In A. Lorde, *Sister Outsider: Essays and Speeches by Audre Lorde*, 114–123. Trumansburg: The Crossing Press.

Lukes, S. 1974, 2005. *Power: A Radical View.* UK: Palgrave McMillan.

Maton, K., and D. Salem. 1995. "Organizational Characteristics of Empowering Community Settings: A Multiple Case Study Approach," *American Journal of Comunity Psychology* 23: 631. Retrieved August 5, 2010, from Research Library. (Document ID: 9345907)

McLoughlin. 1978. *Revivals, Awakenings, and Reform.* Chicago: University of Chicago Press.

Moody, A. 1968. *Coming of Age in Mississippi.* New York: Dell Publishing.

Morrison, T. 1990. "The Site of Memory." In M. Gever, T. Minh-ha, and C. West, eds., *Out There: Marginalization and Contemporary Cultures,* 299–305. Cambridge: MIT Press.

Morrison, T. 1992. *Playing in the Dark: Whiteness and the Literary Imagination.* Cambridge: Harvard University Press.

Nahn, M. 1956. *The Artist As Creator.* Baltimore: Johns Hopkins University Press.

Naido, K., and S. Bannerjee. 2010. "Civil Society." In R. Couto, ed., *Political and Civic Leadership: A Reference Handbook* (vol. 1), 37–46. Sage.

Patterson, O. 1982. *Slavery and Social Death.* Cambridge: Harvard University Press.

Perkins, D. 1995. "Speaking Truth to Power: Empowerment Ideology As Social Intervention and Policy," *American Journal of Community Psychology* 23 (5): 765–794.

Perkins, D. 2010. Empowerment. In R. Couto, ed., *Political and Civic Leadership: A Reference Handbook* (vol. 1), 207–218. Thousand Oaks: Sage.

Perkins, D., and M. Zimmerman. 1995. "Empowerment Theory, Research, and Application," *American Journal of Community Psychology* 23 (5): 569–579.

Piirto, J. 2004. *Understanding Creativity.* Scottsdale: Great Potential Press.

Polyani, M. 1967. *The Tacit Dimension.* New York: Double Day.

Puccio, G., M. Murdock, and M. Mance. 2007. *Creative Leadership.* Thousand Oaks: Sage.

Rappaport, J. 1981. "In Praise of Paradox: A Social Policy of Empowerment over Prevention," *American Journal of Community Psychology* 9: 1–25.

Rappaport, J. 1984. "Studies in Empowerment: Introduction to the Issue," *Prevention in Human Services* 3: 1–7.

Reed-Danahay, D. 1997. *Auto/Ethnography.* New York: Berg.

Schön, D. 1983. *The Reflective Practitioner: How Professionals Think in Action.* USA: Basic Books.

Schultz, A. 1962. *Collected Papers.* The Hague: Nijhoff.

Scott, J. 1985. *Weapons of the Weak: Everyday Forms of Peasant Resistance.* Hartford: Yale University Press.

Scott, J. 1990. *Domination and the Arts of Resistance: Hidden Transcripts.* New Haven: Yale University Press.

Smith, M. 2003. "Micheal Polyani and Tacit Knowledge. The Encyclopedia of Informal Education." Retrieved from www.infed.org/thinkers/polyani.htm.

Solomon, B. 1976. *Black Empowerment: Social Work in Oppressed Communities.* New York: Columbia University Press.

Solomon, B. 1982. "The Delivery of Mental Health Services to African Americans and Their Families: Translating Theory to Practice," In B. Bass, G. Wyatt, and G. Powell, eds., *The*

Afro-American Family: Assessment, Treatment, and Research Issues, 165–181. New York: Grune and Stratton, Inc.

Stallybrass, P., and A. White. 1986. *The Politics and Poetics of Transgression.* Ithaca: Cornell University Press.

Stauffer, J. 2006. Foreword. In Z. Trodd, ed., *American Protest Literature*, xi–xvii. Cambridge: Belknap Press of Harvard University.

Steinbeck, J. 1955, 1976. In G. Plimpton, *Writers at Work : The Paris Review Interviews*, 183. New York: Viking.

Sternberg, R., and T. Lubart. 1999. "The concept of Creativity: Prospects and Paradigms." In R. Sternberg, ed., *Handbook of Creativity,* 3–15. Cambridge: Cambridge University Press.

Swift, C., and G. Levin. 1987. "Empowerment: An Emerging Mental Health Technology," *Journal of Primary Prevention* 8: 71–94.

Taussig, M. 1986. *Shamanism, Colonialism, and the Wild Man: A Study in Terror and Healing.* Chicago: University of Chicago Press.

Thompson, E. 1963. *The Making of the English Working Class.* New York: Pantheon Books.

Tönnies, F. 1926. The Concept of Gemeinschaft. In W. Cahnman and R. Heberle, eds., *Ferdinand Tönnies on Sociology: Pure, Applied, and Empirical,* 62–72. Chicago: The University of Chicago Press.

Trodd, Z. 2006. Introduction. In Z. Trodd, ed., *American Protest Literature.* Cambridge: Harvard University Press.

Vickers, G. 1978. Unpublished Memorandum. MIT. cited in Schon 1983.

Wallas, G. 1926, 1976. "Stages in the Creative Process." In A. Rothenberg and C. Hausman, eds., *The Creativity Queston,* 69–72. Durham: Duke University Press.

West, C. 1991. The Dilemma of the Black Intellectual. In b. hooks and C. West, *Breaking Bread: Insurgent Black Intellectual Life,* 131–146) Cambridge: South End Press.

West, C. 1999a. "Black Strivings in a Twilight Civilization." In C. West, *The Cornel West Reader*, 87–118. New York: Basic Civitas Books.

West, C. 1999b. "The New Cultural Politics of Difference." In C. West, *The Cornel West reader*, 119–139. New York: Basic Civitas Books.

West, C. 1999c. "Prophetc Christian As Organic Intellectual: Martin Luther King, Jr." In C. West, *The Cornel West reader*, 425–434. New York: Basic Civitas Books.

Zinn, H. 2005. *A People's History of the United States: 1942–present*, 2nd ed. New York: Harper Perennial Modern Classics.

www.ingramcontent.com/pod-product-compliance
Lightning Source LLC
Chambersburg PA
CBHW020435290526
45785CB00002B/857